Betel and Miang

Betel and Miang
Vanishing Thai Habits

P. A. Reichart H. P. Philipsen

White Lotus
Bangkok Cheney

This book is dedicated to the people of Thailand

White Lotus Co., Ltd
G.P.O. Box 1141
Bangkok 10501
Thailand

Printed in Thailand

Typeset by COMSET Limited Partnership

ISBN 974-8496-53-8 pbk. White Lotus Co., Ltd., Bangkok
ISBN 1-879155-61-3 pbk. White Lotus Co., Ltd., Cheney

Acknowledgements

The making of this book would not have been possible without the generous assistance of many people to whom the authors are deeply indebted. During our many stays in Thailand from 1984 to 1991 we have received valuable advice, guidance and support from our good colleagues and friends: Dr Aree Jainkittivong, Bangkok, who did a marvellous job in tracing and translating articles written in Thai; Drs Mallika Sookasem, Mingkwan and Piya Vanakul, Sampan Srisuwan and Sirih Poonpipatgul, Chiang Mai, who took us to museums, markets and hill tribe villages and who, thanks to their knowledge of the local scene, introduced us to interesting places we would otherwise never have seen and to knowledgeable people we would never have met.

In Chiang Mai we also received invaluable help from Dr Penth and Messrs Lorenz Ferrari and Horst Schneider. We are very grateful to Mrs A. Maneesinn and Mrs Jettli White who kindly allowed us to photograph parts of their collections of betel utensils. Professor Dr U. Mohr, Hannover, and Drs J. Bautze and G. Venske, Berlin, were very supportive and helpful when it came to matters within their line of expertise.

Special thanks go to Elke Vornheder and Mary Ann Shiffman, Berlin, Grace Hung and Alice Wong, Hong Kong and Vibeke Duch Jensen, Aarhus, Denmark for excellent secretarial and technical assistance. In particular, we are most grateful to Ms Susan Faircloth whose editing and proofreading was most professional and competent. We would not have considered publishing this book were it not for the excellent photographic work provided patiently and meticulously by Josef Eckert, Berlin. We are very grateful to Wolfgang Lorenz, Berlin, who did a marvellous job with the layout, and to our publisher, Mr D. Ande, Bangkok, whose excellent advice and professionalism gave us confidence during the book production.

We wish to thank Freie Universität, Berlin, Deutscher Akademischer Austauschdienst (DAAD), Bonn-Bad Godesberg, the Royal Dental College, Aarhus and the Medical Research Council, Copenhagen, Denmark and the University of Hong Kong for financially supporting our travels to Thailand. Several museums, societies and libraries in Thailand, Germany and Denmark have supplied us with valuable material for which we are most grateful.

Last but not least, we owe gratitude to our respective wives, Barbara Reichart and Kirsten Philipsen for their constant encouragement and support, during the many years of research and frequent travelling to Thailand.

Peter A. Reichart
Hans P. Philipsen
November 1995

Contents

List of Illustrations

1. The Origin of the Betel Chewing Habit

The custom of betel quid chewing is a habit of great antiquity and one which for many centuries has been part of the daily life of probably one-tenth or more of the human race. To a large proportion of the people of Southeast Asia it has in its many nuances been a faithful companion throughout life. It has been there to welcome them into the world, to guard them in childhood, to see them safely married and to accompany them into the next world. Or, as Penzer (1952) puts it in his essay, "The Romance of Betel-chewing": "What other object in existence can boast of such devoted service to man?"

The geographical area covered by the betel chewing habit can be taken as lying roughly between longitude 68° and 178° East and latitude 30° North and 20° South (Fig. 1). Outside this area the custom occurs only where the existence of an Asian colony has warranted the importation of the necessary ingredients of the quid (areca nut, betel leaf and slaked lime). There is no equivalent habit in the Western world.

Where did the habit originate? This is a question which is difficult if not impossible to answer. There are many schools of thought regarding the origin, some favouring the Philippines or Indonesia and others the subcontinent of India and Sri Lanka as the birthplace. Etymological evidence, however, seems to favour an Austro-Asiatic, rather than an Indo-Aryan home. Thus, the origin should be looked for in the Philippines, Sulawesi (Celebes), Kalimantan (Borneo), Java or Sumatra (Penzer, 1952).

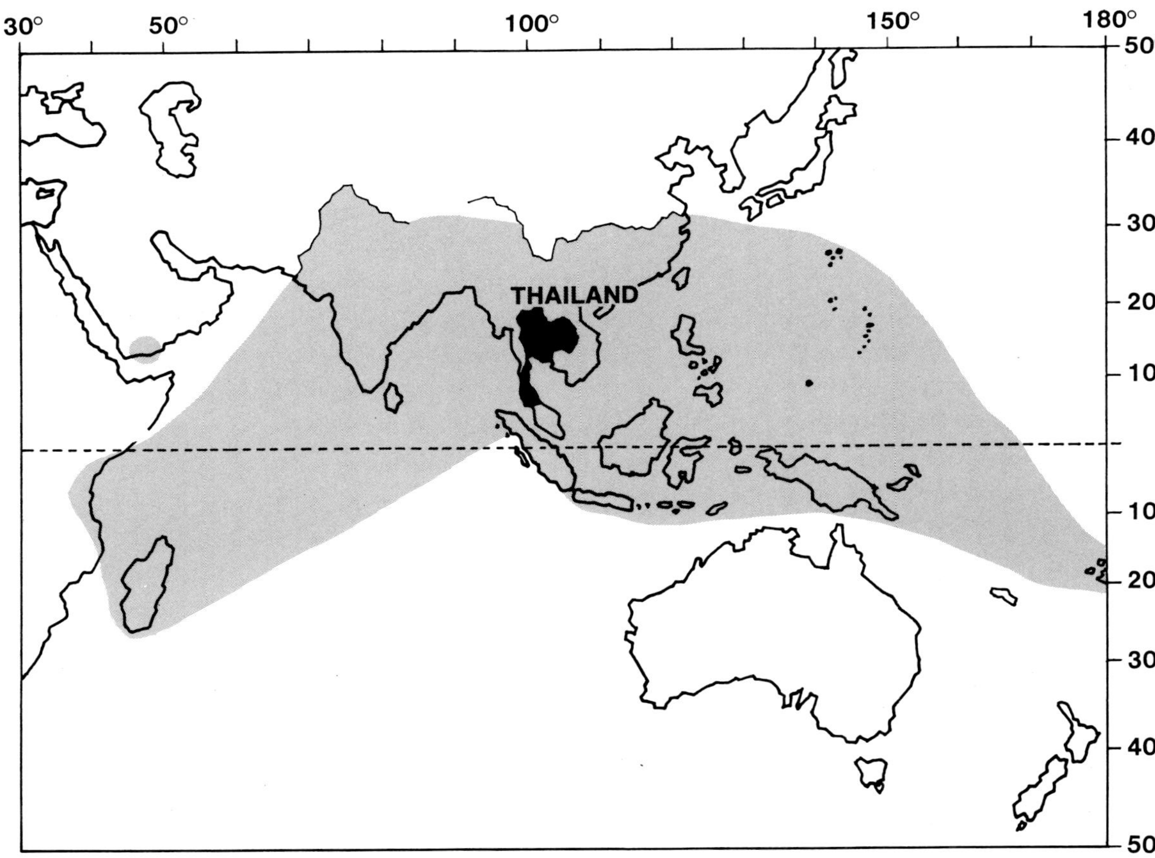

Fig. 1: Map of Southeast and South Asia showing the geographical distribution of the betel chewing habit. Thailand is marked in black (modified after Krenger, 1942).

Archaeological work on prehistoric sites in Southeast Asia has recently shed some light on the probable origin of the betel habit. Traces of piper seeds (probably Piper betle) and of areca have been found in the spirit caves in Northwest Thailand at levels datable to between 5500 and 7000 BC, a period possibly pre-dating the invention of systematic agriculture (Brownrigg, 1991).

How did the custom arise? To answer this question one must consult one of several similar legends which are told in many locations in Southeast Asia. While travelling in the then French Laos during the late 1930s, Ruth Masters Rickover (1975) came across this version in Tonkin:

> But, as often happens in stories, one day they met a beautiful girl with whom both fell in love. She did not know which one she should marry, for in Tonkin, younger sons and daughters may not marry until the older ones have. It would, therefore, have been improper for her to fall in love with the younger brother. But she could not determine which was the older, nor would anyone tell her. In order to discover the firstborn, she resorted to ruse. One day she brought them two bowls of rice, but only one pair of chopsticks. Then she hid behind a curtain and watched. When they had finished eating, she came out blushing and smiling and pointed to one brother saying she loved him and wanted to marry him. He was the one who had eaten first.
>
> The young pair lived happily and so great was their devotion that they completely forgot the twin brother, who had lost both his love and his brother. This made him so sad that he no longer considered life worthwhile and he became a wanderer. Finally he came to a wide river where there was no ferry to take him across. This was the final straw and he could not endure his fate any further so he sat down and died of a broken heart. The gods turned him into a pillar of limestone.
>
> After a while the two lovers came out of their trance and noticed the absence of the twin brother. Remorse shook the young husband and he immediately set off to find his brother, coming in due time to the same river, where he sat down and contemplated his thoughtlessness toward his brother. This broke his heart, and he died and was turned by the gods into an areca palm.
>
> The young wife waited and waited but, as neither the husband nor the twin brother returned to her, she went after them, came to the river, sat down thinking sadly of her wasted life, and also died of a broken heart. The gods turned her into a betel vine growing between the limestone and the areca palm and embracing both as she climbed upwards.
>
> Eventually the story of these unhappy young people reached the ear of the emperor, who decided to search for them. He set out with an army of retainers, at last reaching the same river, where he sat down beside the limestone shaft, while his men built a raft to cross the river. Accidentally, he rubbed a nut from the areca palm against a leaf from the betel vine and touched the limestone with his hand. He noticed the deep red juice on the rock, and in a flash the whole sad tale was revealed to him. He decreed that, in memory of the three unhappy young people, all the inhabitants of the country should rub limestone, areca nut, and the betel vine together and chew the mixture. Since everyone liked the pleasant feeling this left in the mouth, it became the law of the land and was enthusiastically obeyed throughout the realm.

So widespread a custom can be explained only by the fact that it must have had a long history. Only continued use of the betel quid over many centuries can have resulted in so vast a distribution and penetration of the habit into all social classes, as will be described in the following chapters.

In 1298, Marco Polo, the first European explorer to comment on the habit of betel chewing, wrote in his travelogues: "The people of India have a habit of keeping in their mouth a certain leaf called the tembul" (Raghavan and Baruah, 1958). The habit is known to have reached the Zanzibar coast between AD 1200 and 1400, and mention is made in Dutch archives of 1664 from Malacca (West Malaysia) of a tax on betel leaf imported from India. Westerners, unaware of the significant part the habit played in the cultural fabric of the East, were appalled by its use. Tennent (1859) wrote, while staying in Ceylon (Sri Lanka):

> The chewing of these nuts with lime and the leaf of the betel-piper supplies to the people of Ceylon the same enjoyment which tobacco affords to the inhabitants of other countries; but its use is, if possible, more offensive, as the three articles, when combined, colour the saliva of so deep a red that the lip and teeth appear as if covered with blood. Yet, in spite of this disgusting accompaniment, men and women, old and young, from morning till night indulge in this expensive luxury.

During the centuries the chewing of a betel quid has been a delicacy to rich people, to the poor, however, a substitute for food and a stimulant to cope with harsh living conditions.

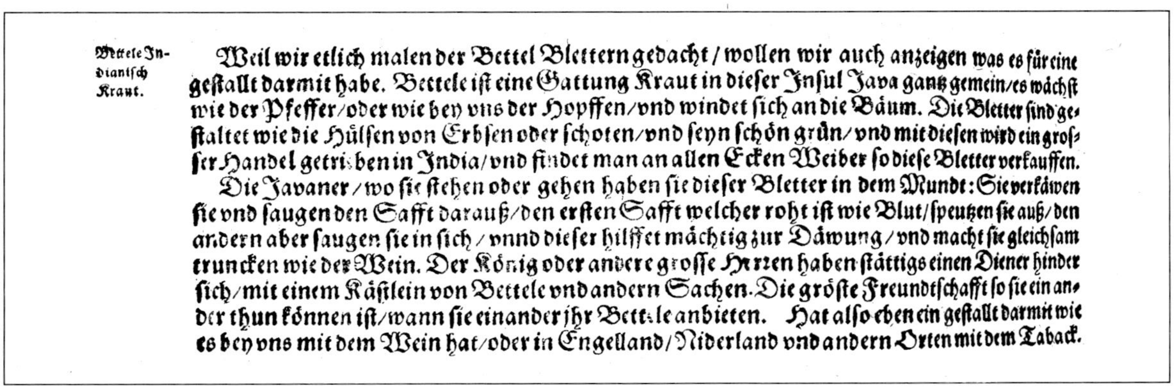
Bettele Indianiſch Kraut.

Weil wir etlich malen der Bettel Blettern gedacht / wollen wir auch anzeigen was es für eine geſtallt darmit habe. Bettele iſt eine Gattung Kraut in dieſer Inſul Java gantz gemein / es wächſt wie der Pfeffer / oder wie bey vns der Hopffen / vnd windet ſich an die Bäum. Die Bletter ſind geſtaltet wie die Hülſen von Erbſen oder ſchoten / vnd ſeyn ſchön grün / vnd mit dieſen wird ein groſſer Handel getriben in India / vnd findet man an allen Ecken Weiber ſo dieſe Bletter verkauffen.

Die Javaner / wo ſie ſtehen oder gehen haben ſie dieſer Bletter in dem Mundt: Sie verkäwen ſie vnd ſaugen den Safft darauß / den erſten Safft welcher roht iſt wie Blut / ſpeutzen ſie auß / den andern aber ſaugen ſie in ſich / vnnd dieſer hilffet mächtig zur Däwung / vnd macht ſie gleichſam truncken wie der Wein. Der König oder andere groſſe Herren haben ſtättigs einen Diener hinder ſich / mit einem Käſtlein von Bettele vnd andern Sachen. Die gröſte Freundtſchafft ſo ſie ein ander thun können iſt / wann ſie einander jhr Bettele anbieten. Hat alſo eben ein geſtallt darmit wie es bey vns mit dem Wein hat / oder in Engelland / Niderland vnd andern Orten mit dem Taback.

Fig. 1.1: Description of the betel-chewing habit from India and Java, in Cosmographia, oder Beschreibung der gantzen Weltt *by Sebastian Münster (Basel, 1628). p. 1606.*

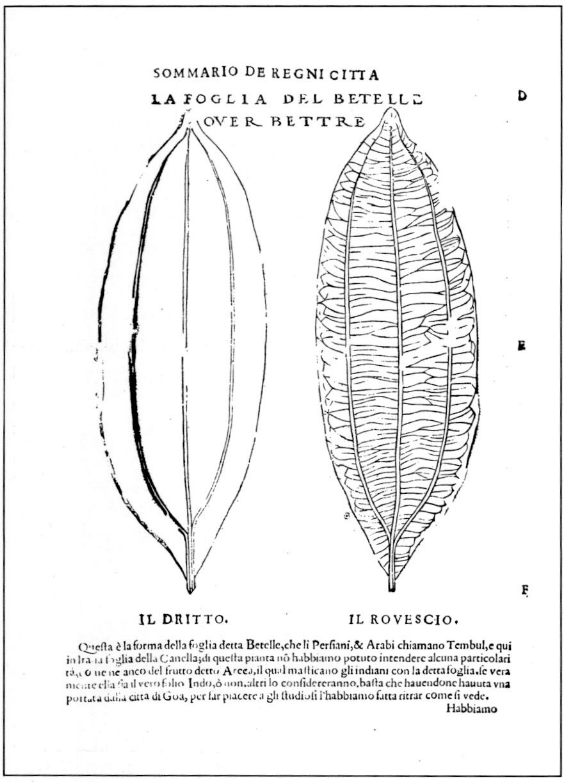

Fig. 1.2: The oldest known woodcut of the betel leaf, published in 1558 by Giovanni Batista Ramusio, who included the report of Duarte in his Delle navigationi et viaggi *(Venice, p. 338).*

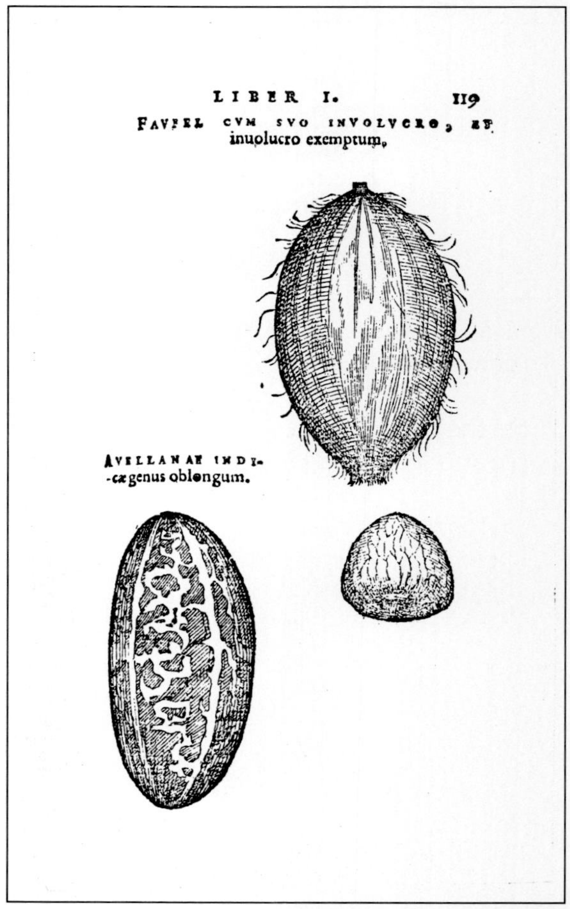

Fig. 1.3: Earliest depiction of the areca nut and fruit (right side of print), published by Carolus Clusius in his Aromatum et simplicium aliquot medicamentorum apud indos nascentium historia *(D. Garcia da Orta, Antwerp, 1567, p. 119).*

2. The Betel Quid

Hobson-Jobson (1886) describes the betel quid as follows:

The leaf of the *Piper betel, L.*, chewed with the dried areca-nut (which is thence improperly called *betel-nut*, a mistake as old as Fryer—1673—see p. 40), *chunam*, etc., by the natives of India and the Indo-Chinese countries. The word is Malayal *vettila*, i.e. *veru+ila*='simple as a mere leaf,' and comes to us through Abbé Port, *betre* and *betle*. **Pawn** (q.v.) is the term more generally used by modern Anglo-Indians. In former times the *betel-leaf* was in S. India the subject of a monopoly of the E. I. Co.

1298.—"All the people of this city (Cael) as well as of the rest of India, have a custom of perpetually keeping in the mouth a certain leaf called *Tembul* . . . . the lords and gentlefolk and the King have these leaves prepared with camphor and other aromatic spices, and also mixt with quicklime . . . ."—*Marco Polo*, ii. 358. See also *Abdurrazzāk*, in *India in XI. Cent.*, p. 32.

1498.—In Vasco da Gama's *Roteiro*, p. 59, the word used is *atombor*, i.e. *al-tamb_l* (Arab.) from Skt. *tāmb_la*. See also Acosta, p. 139. [see **TEMBOOL**.]

1510.—"This betel resembles the leaves of the sour orange, and they are constantly eating it."—*Varthema*, p. 144.

1516.—"We call this betel Indian leaf."—*Barbosa*, 73.

[1521.—'**Bettre** or **vettele**)." See under **ARECA**.]

1552.—". . . . at one side of the bed. . . stood a man . . . who held in his hand a gold plate with leaves of **betelle** . . ."—*De Barros*, Dec. I. liv. iv. cap. vii.

1563.—"We call it **betre**, because the first land known by the Portuguese was Malabar, and it comes to my remembrance that in Portugal they used to speak of their coming not to *India*, but to Calecut . . . . insomuch that in all the names that occur, which are not Portuguese, are Malabar, like **betre**."—*Garcia*, f. 37*g*.

1582.—The transl. of *Castañeda* by N. L. has **betele** (f. 35), and also **vitele** (f. 44).

1585.—A King's letter grants the revenue from betel (**betre**) to the bishop and clergy of Goa.—In *Arch. Port. Or.*, fasc. 3, p. 38.

1615.—"He sent for Coco-Nuts to give the Company, himselfe chewing **Bittle** and lime of Oyster-shels, with a Kernell of Nut called *Arracca*, like an Akorne, it bites in the mouth, accords rheume, cools the head, strengthens the teeth, & is all their Phisicke."—Sir T. Roe, in Purchas, i. 537; [with some trifling variations in Foster's ed. (Hak. Soc.) i. 19].

1623.—"Celebratur in universo oriente radix quaedam vocata **Betel**, quam Indi et reliqui in ore habere et mandere consueverunt, atque ex eâ mansione mire recreantur, et ad labores tolerandos, et ad languores discutiendos . . . . videtur autem esse et *narcoticis*, quia magnopere denigrat dentes."—Bacon, *Historia Vitae et Mortis*, ed. Amst. 1673, p. 97.

1672.—"The pass the greater part of the day in indolence, occupied only with talk, and chewing **Betel** and Areca, by which means their lips and teeth are always stained."—*P. di Vincenzo Maria*, 232.

1677.—The Court of the E. I. Co. in a letter to Ft. St. George, Dec. 12, disapprove of allowing "Valentine Nurse 20 Rupees a month for diet, 7 Rs. for house-rent, 2 for a cook, 1 for **Betle**, and 2 for a Porter, which is a most extravagant rate, which we shall not allow him or any other."—*Notes and Exts.*, No. i p. 21.

1727.—"I presented the Officer that waited on me to the Sea-side (at Calaicut) with 5 zequeens for a feast of **bettle** to him and his companions."—*A. Hamilton*, i. 306.

Compared to other stimulants the betel quid is exceptional in that it is composed of *several* ingredients. Hartwich (1911) distinguishes between components of first, second and third order. First order components are the areca nut, the betel leaf and the lime and these three ingredients together may be regarded as the betel quid in the strict sense. Second order components are catechu and tobacco, the latter being in itself a stimulant. Thus, the addition of tobacco to the quid, as is common in many areas of the betel zone (Fig. 1), produces a combination of several stimulants. Components of the third order comprise a large number of spicy ingredients such as cardamom, cloves, grated fresh coconut, aniseseed and ginger. One or several of these may be added depending on personal taste, local customs and the socio-economic status of the betel quid chewer. Although the chewing of betel quid is practised in several different ways in various countries of the Far East, the major components are relatively consistent. In the following the first and second order components will be described in some detail.

The **areca nut** (often incorrectly named betel nut) is strictly speaking the seed of the fruit of the Areca catechu L. palm tree. Areca is a small genus comprising about 20 species of slender palms of the Palmaceae family. The areca palm is native to South Asia and is found throughout South and Southeast Asia and in several Pacific islands. It is a handsome palm with a tall unbranched, slender stem crowned by a tuft of large, elegant leaves (Fig. 2). It may grow to a height of up to 30 metres. A Thai painting of the nineteenth century nicely depicts the harvesting of the areca nuts, showing the slender areca palms (Fig. 3). The fruits develop in large clusters at the base of the leaves, and vary in size and shape. The fruit is orange-yellow in colour when ripe and is generally the size of a walnut (Fig. 4). The fibrous pericarp or husk is separated from the seed which is then sold in the market as areca or betel nut either fresh, sun dried, or boiled in salt water. By itself the areca nut is

Fig. 2: Areca palm trees with clusters of green areca fruits (Sansai district, Chiang Mai province).

Fig. 3: Harvesting cocoa and betel nuts. Painting on cotton, school of Ratanakosin, c. 1860, former collection J. A. H. Thompson, Bangkok. Reprinted from Boisselier, 1976, p. 62.

highly acidic and astringent to the taste. When used as part of the betel quid the areca nut is sliced or cut into small pieces which are then wrapped in a leaf of betel pepper.

The **betel vine** (Piper betle L.) belongs to a large genus of woody climbers found in all the moist, warm parts of the world (Fig. 5). Several species furnish pepper and other similar spices. It needs careful cultivation and is often grown in shaded gardens. Plucking of leaves is done in the morning and when plucked, the leaves are protected from the sun to preserve the aroma. Fresh betel leaves are bright green in colour and around 15 cm in length. Betel leaves are chewed either in their natural green state or after they have been fermented by being placed in baskets where they are kept damp and dark for from 8 to 24 days.

The third main ingredient of the betel quid—**slaked lime**—is prepared either from seashells, harvested along coastal areas, or from quarried limestone. It is manufactured on an industrial scale and is sold as a paste mixed with water to release calcium hydroxide. The user smears a dab of lime onto

Fig. 4: Several ripe areca fruits with husk, one cut open revealing the nut used for chewing (Chiang Mai, Thailand).

the betel leaf with a finger or a small spatula prior to folding it into a quid. In order to stop the lime from drying out the user may add coconut oil. In some locations in Sri Lanka and Thailand the lime is often tinted pink or yellow with turmeric water.

Tobacco (Nicotina tobacum) is commonly added to the betel quid. This type of smokeless or chewing tobacco is usually sun-cured, and the leaves are cut into strips of various sizes and then often fermented for a short period. There are, however, areas within the betel zone—such as Papua New Guinea— where tobacco is rarely, if ever, used as part of the quid.

Catechu or cutch, a resinous extract from the matrix of the Acacia tree (A. catechu or A. suma) is a common quid ingredient in large parts of India and in Sri Lanka. Due to its high concentration of tannin, it gives astringency to the betel quid. The extract is sun-dried and is usually sold as egg-sized, black lumps. The main ingredients of a betel quid as used in Northern Thailand are shown in Figure 6.

Gambir is a similar substance made from the leaves and young shoots of the shrub Uncaria gambir. The delicacy of flavour of this product depends on its catechin content. It is commonly used in Indonesia and Malaysia as a quid ingredient.

The use of the third order quid components mentioned earlier varies considerably from area to area within the betel zone. These ingredients comprise a wide range of spices, including cloves, fennel, turmeric, saffron, cumin, coriander, nutmeg, cardamom, cinnamon and ginger. Expensive camphor was once quite popular and was thought to be an aphrodisiac. Menthol in crystalline form is a fairly recent additive. It gives the quid a very strong aroma. Lastly, seeds from various melons and cucumber, syrup, rosewater and grated fresh coconut may add a final touch to the betel quid.

The preparation of a betel quid is associated with the use of several utensils or appliances. The tools vary considerably in form, construction and artistic presentation from country to country and from area to area within the betel zone. A detailed description of the utensils will be given in Chapters 9 and 10.

After preparation of the quid it is placed in the mouth, usually between the cheek and the teeth (Fig. 7). The quid is pushed from one side of the mouth to the other, chewed, and pressed against or between the teeth in order to squeeze out the juice. The chewing of a quid causes continuous salivation and the saliva is turned bright red, hence the bloody gouts that spatter roads and pavements in countries where betel chewing is practised. The red colour is produced when certain substances within the areca nut released during chewing come in contact with the strongly alkaline lime. The quid is not swallowed, but is eventually spat out.

Generally, the quid is chewed after meals, and on all auspicious occasions. The number of quids taken per day by regular chewers ranges from two to 15–20. A quid usually lasts for approximately half an hour. Heavy chewers keep the quid in the mouth while sleeping. The quids are not always prepared *ex tempore*. On the Indian subcontinent and in Sri Lanka ready prepared quids are displayed at home on betel stands or kept in the so-called betel bag.

While the basic ingredients of the betel quid are almost the same throughout the entire geographic domain of betel quid chewing, many who have studied the habit over the decades have noted considerable diversity in the art of preparing a quid. A rather crude way of practising the habit was described by Krenger (1942):

In people of Santa Cruz islands, a whole betel nut and several betel leaves are put into the mouth. The gums and the interior of the cheeks are then painted with lime, using an index finger as a spatula.

In large parts of the subcontinent of India and in Sri Lanka betel chewing is prevalent to this day, even in the large cities, and extremely diverse patterns of habit practice are known. In a survey conducted by Balendra (1949) on patients at the Dental Institute in Colombo and others in various parts of the island, it was found that 26 per cent chewed betel quids occasionally, 32 per

Fig. 5: A betel vine climbing the stem of a young areca palm tree. The shape of the fresh light green leaves is characteristic.

Fig. 6: Fermented betel leaf with major betel quid components as used in Northern Thailand. Areca nut, goh bark, catechu and pink lime are used in addition to tobacco (not shown) (Chiang Mai, Thailand).

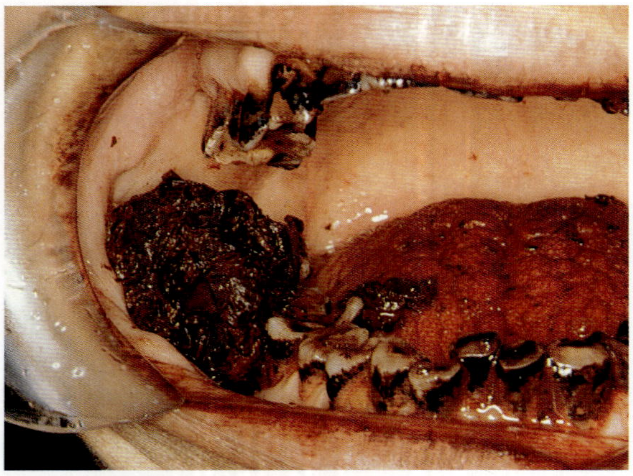

Fig. 7: The mouth of a betel chewer. The betel quid is located between the teeth and the inside of the cheek. Staining of tongue, lips and teeth is typical (Karen hill tribe, Omkoi district).

cent regularly and 12 per cent excessively (almost day and night). In the Hindi language the betel leaf is known as *pan* and the areca nut as *supari*, derived from Sanskrit *supariya* meaning pleasant. In India 13 additives have been mentioned with different medicinal and stimulatory action. In some parts of Papua New Guinea the different constituents of the quid are mixed and taken into the mouth as a paste-like mass without any further conditioning. In the Philippines the quid or *buyo* consists of a betel leaf smeared with lime and rolled or folded so that both ends of the leaf are joined together. In this way, the quid obtains the form of a small boat into which pieces of the areca nut may be deposited. The Malays often give an oblong form to their quids. It appears to be a general habit to remove the tip of the betel leaf before it is served. One legend concerns a young prince with an illness for which no medicine seemed to help (Grabowsky, 1888). A serpent holding a betel leaf in its mouth appeared before him. Recognising this as a gift sent by the gods, the prince first removed the tip of the leaf to avoid swallowing the snake's venom, then chewed it—and recovered. Removing the main vein of the leaf is also rooted in myth, as an Indian king allegedly died from a poisoned hair hidden in the vein of a betel leaf. Wirz (1934) reports that the Gogodara of Papua New Guinea always removed the tip of the betel leaf because they feared injuries to their stomach. While there may be practical reasons for removing the vein, the stem and the tip of the betel leaf—they may simply be too tough to chew—religio-magical aspects may also be decisive. According to Prunner (1966) the Burmese consider the stem of a betel leaf to be the seat of a demon and the tip that of a deity.

Fig. 7.1: Areca palm (right side of print) with flowers and fruit. Published in Neueste Länder-und Völkerkunde. Ein geographisches Lesebuch für alle Stände. Elfter Band. Asien, *Diesbachische Buchdruckerey, Prag, 1812.*

Fig. 7.2: Piper betel as published by Curtis, S. in Botanical Magazine; or Flower Garden Displayed etc. *Vol VI, London, 1832, pl. 3132.*

3. Socio-Ritual Aspects

In 1966 Burton-Bradley, an ethno-psychiatrist, in a paper on Papua New Guinea transcultural psychiatry, concluded that the general literature on betel chewing per se is voluminous.

> Suffice it to say that the rich variety of social functions associated with the custom has been dealt with in a comprehensive fashion by Krenger (1942), Penzer (1952), Raghavan et al. (1958) and Lewin (1964). The early anthropologists such as Cayley-Webster (1898), Williamson (1912), Rivers (1914), Chinnery (1922), Lyons (1926) and Williams (1930) made observations on the broader social aspects of betel chewing behaviour. Most likely because of the new emphasis on social structure and function anthropologists would appear to have lost interest in betel chewing.

However, a few monographs focusing on the ethnography of betel utensils and socio-cultural aspects have been published within the last few decades. In 1965 Millot published a book with emphasis on betel utensils from India. Solange Thierry in 1969 published a catalogue entitled: *Le Bétel I. Inde et Asie du Sud-Est* which contains numerous detailed examples of socio-ritual aspects of betel.

Recently, Rooney (1993) published a booklet entitled *Betel Chewing Traditions in South-East Asia*. Betel-chewing traditions and symbolism are nicely described, as are the art associated with betel and disappearance of the habit from some South-East Asian countries. A particularly nice passage addresses the relationship, or lack of one, between the betel chewing and kissing:

> According to Curzon, 'It is to the same practice [betel chewing] that I suppose must be attributed the total absence . . . of that agreeable mark of salutation . . . the kiss. Lips so tainted could hardly embrace.' Cort had a similar impression: 'The imported kiss is not yet in vogue and I do not see that it ever can be until betel is discarded, for at the present, the nose is a more kissable feature of the Siamese face than the mouth.' The 'absence' of the kiss is more likely due to the social attitude of the Thais rather than to the tradition of betel chewing. The traditional form of greeting for the Thais has always been a *wai* executed with the hands held in a prayer-like position, rather than a kiss or a handshake.
>
> Red lips are a desirable mark of beauty in South-East Asia, just as in most parts of the world. A Burmese love song sings of 'lips reddened by betel juice . . .' . Until the advent of lipstick, this look was achieved by chewing betel regularly. Young Burmese girls reddened their lips with betel for 'dressing up' occasions, recalls Khin Myo Chit . . . .Asian women admired and envied the 'red lips' of European ladies. 'The Vermilion Lips, which the Siamese saw in the Pictures of our Ladies which we had carried to this country, made them to say that we must needs have in France, better Betel than theirs,' wrote Simon de la Loubère, envoy of the King of France in the seventeenth century.

It is well recognised that the habit has a significant function in communication between individuals. When a betel quid is offered or accepted, social contact is made and deepened. A similar significance exists in rituals which may be interpreted as formalised communication between humans and gods. The betel leaf and the areca nut have symbolic significance as signs of happiness and fertility, both in their natural form and in artistic presentations.

Morarjee (1974), in a series of monographs on Indian civilisation and culture, devotes one monograph solely to the study of the *tambula* tradition. *Tambula* refers to betel leaves, areca nut and chunam (slaked lime). The exchange of *tambula* among the Hindus has great social and religious significance. Morarjee says this of *tambula bhoga*, the enjoyment of betel chewing:

The betel chewing has become a deep-rooted habit in Indian life through many centuries. Since the seventeenth century, smoking or eating tobacco also came to coexist with tambula as a habit of Indian people but tobacco has gained no religious significance.

In a Sanskrit encyclopaedic work, the "manasollasa", composed by the Calukya King Somesvara II (*c.* AD 1130), tambula was considered one of the eight bhogas of an individual's life. The latter are the "vilepana bhoga" (enjoyment of unguents), the "dhupa bhoga" (enjoyment of incenses), the "yosi bhoga" (enjoyment of women), the "vastropa bhoga" (enjoyment of garments or clothes befitting different seasons), the "sangita vinoda" (enjoyment of music), the "tambula bhoga" (enjoyment of tambula), the "sayya bhoga" (enjoyment of beds), the "anna bhoga" (enjoyment of food), and the "malyopa bhoga" (enjoyment of flowers and garlands). A celebrated poet, Gagabhatta (*c.* AD 1620–1685), also mentions tambula as one of the eight "bhogas" whose details correspond to what is implied in the above mentioned list. The enjoyments mentioned would convince that the Indians of ancient and medieval times took pragmatic interest in material cultural advancement as much as in the spiritual development.

The Hindu Dharmasastras prescribed that only a "grhastha"—a married householder (husband and wife)—is entitled to tambula bhoga, for it is his or her life that was given to "bhoga" or material enjoyment within certain limits. In his remarks on "sayana-vidhi" or use of bed by a householder, commentator Sridhara mentions that the householder should go to bed with his wife after enjoying perfumes and tambula. Betel is chewed after meals and as often as needed by the individual, according to habit. The Astanga-samgraha, a medical treatise written by Vagbhata (*c.* AD 625 or about AD 850) prescribes the use of tambula after getting up from sleep, after meals, after bath, after vomiting etc. This tambula should consist of two betel leaves, one betel nut, chunam and catechu.

According to the Dharmasastras, tambula-bhoga is forbidden to an ascetic (yati), a student (brahmacarin), a dikshita (one initiated for a religious ceremony), a person observing a "vrata" or religious vow, and a person offering funeral oblations—"sradha"—to his ancestors on specific days. These restrictions were obviously imposed with a view to helping the persons concerned to concentrate solely on the objectives of their pursuits, avoiding temptations, stimulants or intoxicants which might detract them from their main goal.

Betel leaves and areca nuts are even today indispensable in many socio-ritual contexts. They are part of ritual offerings and gifts, whether between individuals or as an honour to a god or spirit. Union or disunion, marriage or divorce, contract or rupture—in other words all positive or negative aspects of life—may be accompanied by the ritualised use of the betel quid.

The most common and easily understood usage is that of a quid as a sign of hospitality. Giving and receiving a quid is regarded as a preparation of a good relationship. The sharing and offering of a quid is thus often a standard act of formal greeting. Young, in his book entitled *The Kingdom of the Yellow Robe*, describes this as well as some other aspects of the effects of betel chewing:

> Every caller is offered a tray of betel-nut and its accompanying condiments; a cup of tea, and cigarettes. The betel-nut is not eaten alone, but with a mixture of tobacco, seri-leaf, turmeric and lime, and no host ever forgets to offer these things to his guest. In time, as a result of continual chewing, the gums and lips become a vivid red, and the teeth an intense shiny black, and in extreme old age the teeth also protrude in a repulsive fashion. The first effect of the nut upon a beginner is rather of an intoxicating or stupefying nature. But after having once contracted a strong liking for its bitter flavour, many people find them-

selves absolutely unable to do without it. Every man carries in his pocket a small box containing the nut, the tobacco etc., or is followed wherever he goes by his servant who bears it after him. When the master sits down, the servant deposits it by his side so that it is easily within reach of the owner. These boxes are often of valuable material and beautiful workmanship. The commonest material used in their construction is silver, but the wealthier classes have their betel-boxes made of rich, ruddy gold and set with jewels. The black teeth that are obtained by the constant use of the nut are considered beautiful. The natives express their contempt for white teeth in the remark, "Any dog can have white teeth." The local dentists keep in stock complete sets of black false teeth, so that when a naturally black tooth is removed, an artificially coloured one can at once take its place and so prevent any break in the uniform coal-like aspect of the mouth. Saliva is produced in copious quantities during mastication, and is of a blood red colour. As it is never swallowed, spittoons must always accompany the betel-box. If the saliva is allowed to fall upon wood or stone it produces brick-red stains which are not easily removeable. Such stains are exceedingly common in the streets and houses. The black deposit formed upon the teeth is said to exercise a preserving influence on them.

Receiving, offering and chewing betel quids together is not only a ritualised form of a positive social contact. It may by virtue of the red mouth of a betel chewer indicate that this particular person is doing well and that he or she has been treated nicely as a guest. In contrast to this everyday use in almost all betel chewing societies the ritual form and use is standardised, formalised and has symbolic character. In Northern Bihar in India, in the area of Midhila (Moser-Schmitt, 1981) it is said that gods do not possess betel quids and that therefore humans have to offer these to appease them. *Pan* and *supari*, betel leaf and areca nut, are considered by these people as signs of happiness.

In principle, betel as a gift has many advantages, as was stated by Brownrigg in his 1991 monograph on betel cutters. It is intimate, it is popular at all levels of society, and it suffers from relatively few of the social and religious taboos associated with food, alcohol and tobacco. In this context one may cite the Buddhist clergy. Brownrigg records that Sir George Scott noted that in Burma the Buddhist monks, though forbidden to smoke, are among the most persistent chewers of betel, which is seen as a great stimulator of the meditative faculties. Many travellers have observed and described the rituals and rules associated with the exchange of betel. Brownrigg describes some examples:

> Apart from the outright offence of not offering betel, there were all sorts of nuance of etiquette involved in the exchange, and ample scope for oblique insults. The speed with which the betel box was produced for a visitor might indicate the enthusiasm with which the visit was regarded and the social distance which the host wished to keep. If the box was clearly not the host's best, the guest could draw the obvious conclusion. Among some groups, such as the Hanunoo of the Philippines, conversation could only continue so long as betel continued to be offered; so, if the host produced a small supply which was immediately used up, it was an indication that he did not want the conversation to be a long one. In India, on the other hand, betel was traditionally offered to the guest before departure, and so the sudden appearance of the betel box might indicate that the guest was beginning to outstay his welcome.

Another interesting offering of betel and areca nuts formerly observed in Thailand occurred at the moment of ordination of a monk. In preparing this ceremony small receptacles made of banana leaves had to be made ready, containing the flowers for use during the ceremony. Servants and women busily prepared these containers, others cutting betel nuts and still others rolling the betel leaves. All of this was of great importance in the ordination ceremony (Thierry, 1969).

The social significance of such rituals in India has often been stressed. Morarjee (1974) wrote:

> At the time of betrothal, and in weddings, tambula (betel) is exchanged between the bride and bridegroom sides, signifying agreement and understanding with regard to the terms of marriage and the marriage itself. It is also customary among the Hindus that on social visits, at the time of parting, the tambula is offered by the host to the guest. This seems to be a traditional custom and it is interesting to note that in the "Subhasita-Ratnakara" one Subhasita thus says: "Oh, friend, there are hundreds of thousands [of] good qualities in tambula; there is, however, one immensely bad feature associated with it, namely, the sending away (of guests) after its bestowal."

Over the years the betel quid has played a central role in betrothal and marriage. During the marriage ceremony as it is practised in Northern Bihar in India the bride receives five betel quids which she throws at the feet of her groom who has to pick them up (Moser-Schmitt, 1981). This gesture of antipathy, as it is, is easy to understand if one considers that freedom ends for the Hindu woman when she enters marriage. The significance of the rite is accentuated by the fact that five stylised betel leaf motives are painted on the floor where the ceremony takes place. In a second rite the bride and groom exchange quids and chew together as a sign of sympathy.

Since engagement and marriage are important social functions where the betel quid plays a role a few more examples may illustrate this. In his studies of the cultural history of India, Gode (1960) elaborates on what he calls the amatory perspective of the matrimonial custom of cutting the betel leaf roll. He mentions a specific custom which is practised in Maharashtra during marriage ceremonies: at the dinner bride and groom sit opposite each other. A small roll of betel leaves called *vidi* is then given to the young woman who takes it and holds it between her lips, one part of the roll sticking out of her mouth. At a certain signal from the parents and guests, in a joyous atmosphere the newly weds share the roll by biting into it. Gode saw in this practice a kind of alliance kiss, the only one exposed to the public in Indian society. It is quite evident that the association of betel quids with engagement, betrothal, and marriage is a true element of love.

Engagement and marriage are always accompanied by the gift and exchange of betel. In Thailand the fiancé would always send a *khan mak man,* an engagement bowl of areca nuts, to the girl. It contained six small packets of betel, each packet containing eight betel leaves and six areca nuts. Leaves of other plants were added as well as flowers with such beautiful symbolic descriptions as flower of love or flower of the glittering star. For marriage at least two such bowls had to be offered, prepared in a similar way. According to the status of the young man, the bowl of areca nuts for marriage should be made of gold or silver. First-class bowls, generally those containing gold or a sum of money, thus differed from second-class bowls, which merely contained fruits, powdered sugar and areca nuts. Noble and beautiful ladies would be accompanied by a marriage broker and a servant boy who would carry these bowls as gifts from the young man's family to that of the girl.Tradition has it that betel leaves, areca nuts and powdered sugar had to be distributed to family members and friends. This seems to have been the way of discreetly announcing the happy news. On the day of the marriage ceremony the bowl containing areca nuts would often be handled with solemnity and might be given a special place in the festive procession. Young, in *The Kingdom of the Yellow Robe*, describes the association of the wedding ceremony and "the betel-nut tray"

> At every wedding feast there are always three metallic plates or dishes containing respectively, Chinese cakes, a very highly seasoned kind of mincemeat, and a tray

of betel-nut. These three dishes were formerly known collectively, under the name of "the betel-nut tray," and so universal is the custom of providing them, that the wedding ceremony itself is now frequently spoken of by the same name.

As in India and Thailand, the offering of betel and areca nuts during the ceremonies of engagement and marriage plays a significant role in the rest of Southeast Asia. In Laos, Cambodia, Malaysia and Burma, all neighbours of Thailand, the rituals of offering and receiving betel between the families of the bride and groom are amazingly similar. In Malaysia, for example, the couple to be engaged is called *pinangan,* a term derived from the term for the areca nut, *pinang* in Malay. The representatives of the young man offer a plate of betel to the family of the girl, and both families reunite to take a common meal, which of course is followed by the exchange of betel. One family member of the young man offers the betel, saying: "This is meant for the engagement of your daughter". The father of the girl replies, using a formula of acceptance: "If it is so I will accept the engagement". In Laos during engagement and marriage numerous exchanges of betel unite the two families, being an important part of the formal promise. Offerings carried by young girls to the house of their fiancé consist, of course, of betel and tobacco as a first gift, followed by cakes and other specialities. In Cambodia, according to a story relating to the origin of the dynasties of this country, Prince Prah Thong, the first sovereign of this country, was supposed to have married a serpent princess. Some say that after the first meeting she returned home leaving a betel quid with Prah Thong as a sign of her fidelity.

Birth rites are similarly accompanied by the ceremonial use of betel. When a woman is close to the time of delivery certain rules must be followed scrupulously in order to guarantee the child's safe arrival in this world. In Laos the young mother must make particular invocations, avoid certain gestures, and comb and wash with exceptional care. When the day of delivery comes a plate of offerings is presented to the midwife, and she prostrates herself before the plate, invoking the spirits of the master who taught her the formulas and techniques of midwifery. Using a long rope fixed to the rafters the mother tries to facilitate the descent of the foetus. The midwife massages her, applying the powder of various roots to her belly, and tries to make her vomit, using a betel peduncle. During the forbidden weeks following the birth, when mother and child may become bewitched by evil spirits, a decoction of certain roots and leaves is prepared to re-establish the mother's circulation. In order to guarantee the efficacy of this brew, banana leaves, flowers and—in particular—betel quids are placed on the spot in which it is cooked (Thierry, 1969). In Cambodia in a rite designed to call up the vital spirits, a wise woman applies to the fontanelle a sort of vegetal plaster which must be renewed every two weeks for a period of seven to eight months. Often the midwife proceeds in a solemn fashion, resulting in a family festivity. Having divided a betel leaf into three parts she prepares three quids which consist of only a piece of leaf and a piece of root of a certain type of ginger. One is for herself, the other two are presented to the grandmother and the godmother who immediately chew them. Afterwards the midwife makes a small round hole in a second betel leaf which she places on the baby's cranium, the whole corresponding to the fontanelle. The three women then cover this with the mixture they have chewed. Candles and incense are lighted and the ancestors are invoked, being invited to come and take part of the offering and to bless the descendant. The gods of the ten points of the universe are also invoked, and asked (through the anointment of the betel mixture) to ensure the development of the newborn's fragile cranium.

Betel's association with death and funeral rights is also widespread throughout Southeast Asia. At the moment of the death agony of a parent the members of the family prepare the offerings and food for the monks who will recite during the funeral. A candle, a bowl of betel and a bowl of water are placed close to the head of the dead body. Among the offerings are banana leaves rolled into a packet containing areca nuts, betel leaves and incense. These offerings are not deposited before the monks but placed between the hands of the dying person. This offering is considered to be a viaticum, which in the other world may be offered on a celestial reliquary. Giving and taking betel has thus been a ritual accompanying the whole year and the entire life of the betel chewing society. In Southeast Asia not only Buddhist activities and legal festivals give rise to particular rituals, but private celebrations among parents, friends and neighbours are also occasions where betel could play a role.

In former times betel was of particular significance at court in Southeast Asia and India, as Brownrigg (1991) explains in his monograph on betel cutters. Foreign diplomats have described the importance of betel at the courts of past Asian rulers. Two features are common to these descriptions. Firstly the ruler himself chewed betel throughout the audience. Secondly he offered it from his own tray, or occasionally from his own mouth as a token of favour. An even greater honour than being offered betel was to be offered one of the receptacles which contained it.

In Southeast Asia the identification of betel with monarchy has been particularly close. Betel sets there formed an integral part of the regalia and were a favoured item for diplomatic gifts from one ruler to another. Betel receptacles formed part of the regalia of the Thai kings, the former kings of Burma and the rulers of the Malay States. In Thailand there are several fine betel sets among the regalia and royal heirlooms. When the present crown prince was formally invested one part of the regalia he received consisted of 21 items including a betel set and spittoon, both of enamelled gold.

The red saliva produced during betel chewing may be taken as a sign of salutation or even as a sign of magic. Native people consider it to possess vital force or to be a magic elixir. Thus, the members of the Macassar tribe of Sulawesi paint the forehead and temples of their sick children with a betel chewer's saliva. In the Philippines the bellies of babies are painted with saliva in order to keep them from catching a cold. Many people use the ingredients of a betel quid in their practice of magic and divination. On the island of Timor the holy man paints the forehead and chest of a warrior with betel juice. The colouration that the juice takes as it contacts the skin indicates how the fates will induce power and influence the outcome of the fighting. In Java the pattern of spittings serves to indicate the nature of a sickness and the colour of a spitting signifies traits of character. The Batak of Sumatra fool bad spirits by depositing betel quids at certain locations to keep them from pursuing humans. Also in Java malevolent spirits are kept away by the sight or smell of betel spittings (Thierry, 1969). A medium in Vietnam never enters trance or starts an oracle session after having taken a betel quid. During initiation ceremonies or during exorcism the betel quid itself represents the ritual nourishment. During the five days which precede the mask dances of the Baining of New Britain in Papua New Guinea the dancers are not supposed to take anything but areca nuts and water.

Even during the preparation of a betel quid magic may be involved. In Northern Bihar in India love magic is feared from wives who prepare betel at home to give to their husbands, as is revealed in the following ballad from Bengal: Rangila fetched the betel quid and coloured her lips red. She was still young but knew of witchcraft. She could bewitch the betel quid so that everyone who chewed it immediately left his own wife . . . This ballad concerns the contents of a betel quid which the recipient, trusting the one who gave it, eats or chews with confidence. Given such trust, hashish or—in the past—opium could be hidden in the quid. It is conceivable that aphrodisiacs could have been added to the quid without the recipient knowing it. It is thus easy to understand how the one who was offered the betel quid might have felt enchanted and not reacted normally.

In her book, *Tambula: Tradition and Art* (1974), S. Morarjee described the wide varieties of beliefs associated with the chewing of the betel nut (*tambula*):

> The beliefs associated with tambula have grown through centuries reflecting the attitudes and social relationships among the people. A work on Dharmasastra called the "Jyotirnibandha" attributed to Sivaraja (Sivadasa), composed sometime before AD 1524, contains twenty-four stanzas dealing with tambula. The first two stanzas deal with the auspicious time for chewing tambula according to astrological beliefs. In the third stanza it is said that a mouth devoid of the Veda (Vedic chant), the juice of tambula and witty saying is a mere "bila" i.e. hole! The fourth and fifth stanzas dwell on merits of making gifts of tambula made of good nuts, good betel and chunam to Brahmins. The spiritual manifestation in tambula is hinted [at] in the sixth and seventh stanzas which say that the betel nut pleases Brahma, the betel leaves please Vishnu and the chunam pleases Isa (Siva). Tambula being the manifestation of Brahma, Vishnu and Siva it brings prosperity and good fortune leading to the fulfilment of our desires. Hence a gift of tambula is desirable.
>
> The eighth stanza says that a tambula with one nut is the best, that with two nuts bears no fruit while that with three nuts is exceedingly best. The ninth stanza lays down that a tambula with thirty-two betel leaves should be given to the king, while tambula offered to a tributary prince should contain only twenty-four betel leaves. The tenth stanza enjoins that a tambula to be given to a son-in-law should consist of eighteen betel leaves, to a scholar twelve, and to a bride, ten. The eleventh stanza prescribes that a tambula of eight betel leaves be given to people of our liking while the tambula to be given to ordinary persons should consist of four betel leaves only.
>
> The stanzas thirteen and fourteen deal with the gift of tambula to enemies. The tambula offered to enemies should contain only six betel leaves. A gift of betel-nuts to enemies bears fruit thus: one betel-nut, profit; two betel-nuts, loss; three betel-nuts, pleasure or happiness; four betel-nuts, pain or misery; five betel-nuts, longevity and six betel-nuts, death. The stem of the betel leaf is associated with sin.
>
> According to the fourteenth stanza, the betel leaf which is crumbled destroys human life while the veins of the leaf destroy intellect. The roll of the tambula should be held with its tip pointing upward. A single betel-leaf should be held with its end up.
>
> The stanzas fifteen to twenty-one deal with "do's" and "don'ts" and their consequences. Chewing a tambula with chunam applied to it with one's thumb brings wealth. The eating of the end and stem of a betel-leaf as also two betel leaves with chunam and the eating of a betel-nut without putting a betel-leaf in the mouth produce poverty for seven generations and prevent the realisation of God Vishnu after death. One should not chew tambula without taking chunam with one's forefinger; if done so out of ignorance, the person so doing finds place in hell. If one chews tambula by taking it on his left hand or from the hand of a woman out of ignorance, the prosperity comes to an end. The application of chunam with thumb contributes to success in all directions as it leads to victory, acquisition of woman and garment. The chewing of tambula with essence of catechu by day is quite becoming but the use of catechu for chewing at night will destroy the glory of even Indra.
>
> The stanza twenty-second enumerates the thirteen qualities of tambula mentioned earlier: pungency, bitterness, heat, sweetness, saltiness, astringent flavour, capacity to remove "vata", antiseptic character, capacity to remove phlegm, capacity to stimulate passion and capacity to beautify and purify the mouth, removing all bad odour from it.
>
> The last two stanzas point out that one who chews tambula with preponderance of chunam at midday and pre-

Fig. 8: Portrait of Maharana Pratap Singh, ruler of Mewar (1751–54) holding a betel quid in his right hand (Mewar, India).

Fig. 9: A maid offers betel to a prince and his companion in a winter palace (Kangra, early nineteenth century, India).

> ponderance of betel-leaves at night, attains increasing prosperity. A wise man should always use three parts of betel-nut, two parts of betel-leaf and one part of catechu while preparing tambula.

The betel leaf itself is often associated with a female deity. The leaf having the basic shape of a triangle which is identified as the female genital organ, the vulva, is thus representative of female fertility (Moser-Schmitt, 1981). Like the lotus leaf, the archaic name for which, *purain*, means placenta, and the stem of which is thought to be the umbilicus, the betel leaf and stem may also be compared to the vulva and the placenta. In Northern Bihar the areca nut is called *phal*, meaning fruit. The folded betel leaf contains parts of areca nut which symbolises the male semen. The betel quid thus symbolises the fertilised mother's lap which opens and bears life while leaving the red trace of bleeding behind. In this context it is of interest that Indian miniatures sometimes show as a motive the birth of Krishna on a betel leaf. Indian miniatures from the sixteenth to the nineteenth century often show the exchange of betel quids or the components thereof among royalty (Figs. 8, 9). The significance of the betel quid as a symbol of fertility or its role in combatting female sterility may be illustrated by another example. In the Ratnagiri district in India the best method of countering sterility was to steal a statuette of a Krishna during the celebration of Krishna's birth and replace it with a coconut or an areca nut. In some rural parts of Thailand it is even today customary to pay the midwife for her services with money wrapped inside a betel leaf (Conklin, 1988a).

Fig. 9.1: Indian miniature of the late 17th century in the Mewar style, showing Krishna receiving a betel quid. On the bed several betel quids and a box with betel is also seen (Mewar, seventeenth century).

4. Effects and Side Effects of Betel Quid Chewing

Since the early Indian writings it has been known that chewing of betel quids expels wind, removes phlegm, kills germs and subdues bad odour, beautifies the mouth, removes impurities, and induces love, the last-mentioned effect having been dealt with above. Betel quid chewing is said also to dull the sensation of hunger and to regulate or accelerate digestion by causing increased bowel movements.

Lewin (1964) has supplied us with one of the most colourful descriptions of a Westerner's experience when chewing a betel quid for the first time. He writes:

> Persons not accustomed to the chewing of betel experience a disagreeable, acrid, and burning taste, and a feeling of constriction in the throat after a very short period of mastication. Slight sores on the tongue and the throat also occur. As more betel is chewed, this at first almost intolerable sensation diminishes. Finally, hardly anything of the kind is felt, and the sensations experienced are even agreeable. The perception of taste is not infrequently reduced for a short time, probably on account of the essential oil contained in the leaves, or perhaps the action of the lime. But even if it is possible for Europeans to become accustomed to the taste of betel, there is one circumstance which frequently prevents them from becoming addicted to the drug, and that is the excessive amount of saliva formed, which, especially at the beginning, obliges them to spit very frequently. This is all the more repugnant to Europeans because the saliva is yellowish-brown, brownish-red or blood-red, according to the amount of lime used. This excessive salivation according to my own experiments has its origin in an irritation of the mouth by the ingredients of the areca nut. The colouration of the saliva is also due to the colouring matter of the nut which assumes the hues described under the influence of the alkaline lime. The usual threefold mixture, areca nut, betel leaf and lime, furnishes a red-brown saliva, the four-fold, areca nut, betel leaf, gambir and catechu, and lime a saliva of more blood-red colour. The differences, however, are not great. After the first effects of the excitation of the salivary glands and the irritation of the mucous membranes of the mouth have passed off, a pleasant odour remains in the mouth. This has always been considered one of the charms of betel-chewing. The betel leaf alone does not give rise to this smell. The odour which it produces is aromatic, but not in the least agreeable. It is the areca nut alone to which this effect is due. My experiments proved that an odoriferous substance is formed by the action of the lime on the nut, which in minute quantities has an extremely agreeable flavour. The latter is very lasting if, for instance, a few drops of the concentrated solution in ether are brought in contact with the hands or clothes. In the mouth the same effect can be observed, but to a far less degree. I can well imagine that betel is chewed on account of this odour and agreeable taste. This opinion should not be objected to on the ground that many old and inveterate betel-chewers in Siam exhale an extremely unpleasant breath which, on account of its peculiarity, is called betel smell. It is stated to be so intense that the windward side is preferred when speaking with such people. This pungent smell is caused by the decomposition of small pieces of the morsel stuck between the teeth if the latter are not cleaned. Nevertheless, such persons still experience the agreeable smell and taste developed by the betel quid, and continue to chew betel in spite of the putrefaction in their mouths, or perhaps even, at a later stage, on account of it. Moreover, Jagor never noticed a bad smell from the breath of betel-chewers, and stated that it would be desirable for this custom to exist in Europe also, where foul breath is a frequent evil, especially in older persons.

Fig. 10: Karen hill tribe woman with brownish-red lips and black teeth as a result of betel chewing.

Fig. 11: Lisu, a woman with characteristic costume showing the red-brown lips of a betel chewer.

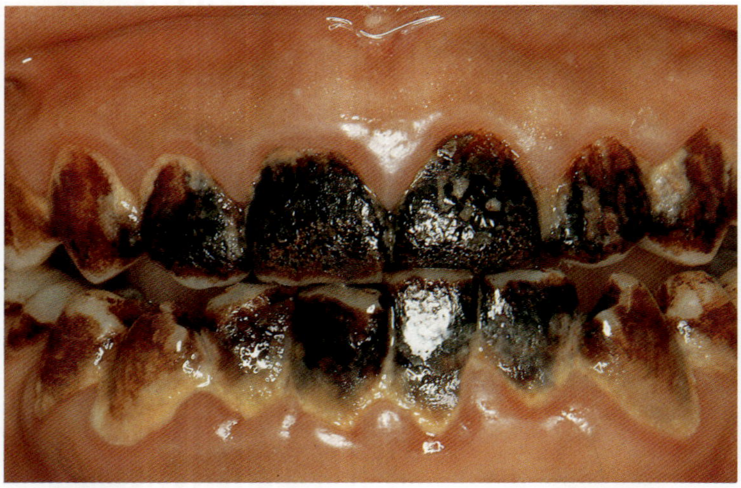

Fig. 12: Black coating of teeth due to polyphenols contained in the areca nut and betel leaves (Doi Saket, Chiang Mai province).

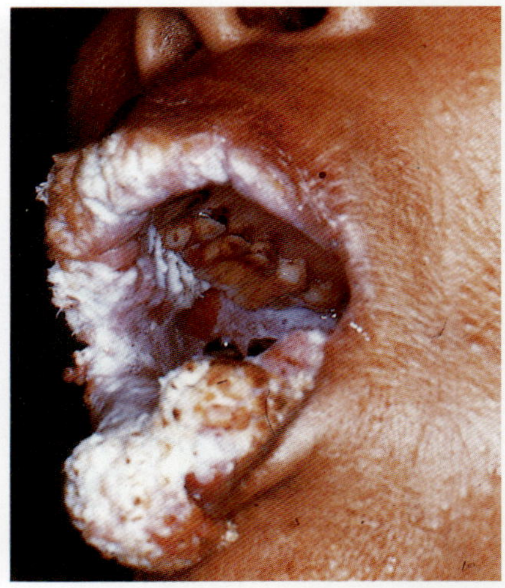

Fig. 14: Extensive mouth cancer (so-called verrucous carcinoma) in a woman who chewed betel quids daily for more than 30 years (Chiang Mai, Thailand).

Fig. 13: Porcelain jar containing toothpaste. The content of the powdered areca nut was believed to contribute to the prevention of dental decay (England, nineteenth century).

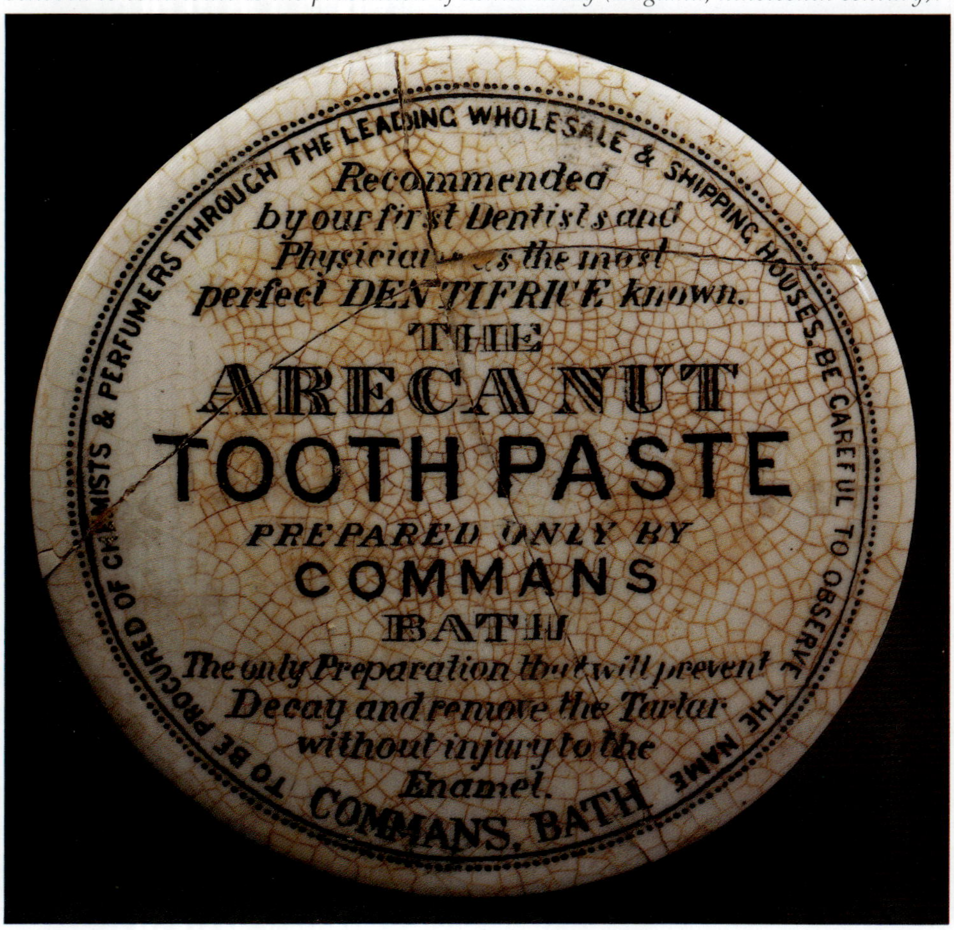

The various **pharmacological (and poisonous)** effects of betel quid chewing are caused by the numerous substances released from the ingredients during chewing. Thus, the areca nut contains a number of active substances such as so-called alkaloids and tannins. The mature green betel leaves contain volatile oils, nitrates, and small quantities of sugar, starch and tannins. Raw tobacco which is often added to the quid contains more than 2,000 substances of which major classes of compounds are aliphatic and aromatic hydrocarbons (carcinogens), phenols, aldehydes, carbohydrates, chlorinated organic compounds, and at least 35 metal compounds.

The **side effects** of betel chewing are quite numerous. It produces effects on the brain and local effects in the mouth where the quid is kept. The nature and intensity of the systemic effect seem to depend on the species and degree of maturity of the nut. The quid can be considered as a mild excitant with narcotic and stimulating properties. The betel quid chewer experiences a feeling of well-being. He is in a good humour and is, according to the statements of Burmese monks, inspired to self-reflection and to work if he has the disposition thereto.

The **local effects** in the mouth are firstly a quite marked attrition or wear of the teeth, with the repeated chewing producing sharp-edged and jagged tooth crowns. The teeth of the chewer are stained black or brownish due to the action of the lime on the alkaloids and tannins contained in the areca nut (Reichart et al., 1985). Among any group of upcountry villagers in Thailand, it is easy to distinguish the betel chewers (Figs. 10, 11).

Secondly, as mentioned earlier, betel quid chewing produces copious salivation which in combination with the poor oral hygiene characteristic of most chewers results in heavy deposition of calculus or tartar around the crowns of teeth. Lewin (1964) reports that in the Admiralty Islands the formation of this tartar is regarded as an attribute of the dignity of a chief, for only the very rich are in a position to indulge so freely in chewing as to produce such quantities of tartar (Fig. 12).

Thirdly, chewing of the quid in combination with poor oral hygiene produces a damaging effect to the gums leading to severe gum disease and looseing of the teeth. The large deposits of calculus may, however, occasionally cement teeth together masking loosened teeth. On the other hand dental decay (caries) seems less pronounced among betel chewers than among non-chewers. This caries-preventing effect may be caused by the high content of fluoride or the presence of antibacterial substances in the betel quid ingredients (Möller et al., 1977). It is interesting that in the nineteenth century areca nuts were used in toothpaste in order to prevent dental decay (Fig. 13). In a recent study (Ettinger et al., 1985) 423 villagers (with mean age of 33 years) living in the eastern part of Thailand were interviewed about dental health beliefs. In spite of the fact that over 90 per cent of the villagers agreed with the statement, "If you clean your gums and teeth regularly, it will prevent oral disease", 73 per cent believed that chewing betel nut routinely protects against oral disease.

Fourthly, but certainly representing *the most harmful side effect*, betel quid chewing may exert a local cancer-producing effect on the oral mucosa (Fig. 14). It is believed that betel quids containing tobacco are the most hazardous in this respect. It has, however, recently been shown that lime may have a uranium isotope content 20 times that of chewing tobacco (Chakarvarti et al., 1981), thus adding yet another factor to the cancer-inducing effect of betel quid ingredients. It is generally agreed that the extraordinarily high incidence of mouth cancer in South and Southeast Asia is causally related to betel quid chewing either alone or in combination with other habits like tobacco smoking. A full account on the hazardous cancer-producing effects of chewing betel on the mucosa of the mouth was given in a monograph published by the International Agency for Research on Cancer under the auspices of the World Health Organisation (1985). Further, a more recent study (Sinor et al., 1990) has shown that the areca nut is the most important aetiological factor in the development of so-called oral submucous fibrosis, a chronic oral precancerous disease leading to stiffness of the oral mucosa and inability to open the mouth.

Fig. 13.1: Piper species (amalago L. and malamiris) as published in Herbarium Amboinense *by G. E. Rumphius, Vol. V. 1747, p. 335.*

5. Early Accounts of Betel Chewing in Siam

Archaeological work on a prehistoric site known as "The Spirit Cave", in Northwest Thailand (from a period between BC 7000 and 5500) has disclosed traces of both seeds, that could very well be those of piper betle, and areca nuts. However, although such evidence suggests that the habit of betel quid chewing is likely to be as ancient in Thailand as in most other oriental countries the first written accord of the habit dates back only about seven hundred years. The famous obelisk or stele of King Rama Khamhaeng (AD 1275–1317) contains an inscription in the earliest known form of Thai script which is interpreted as saying that: "The people of this country of Sukothai set up areca plantations (*pa mak*) and betel plantations (*pa phlu*) all over the country. In this country there are also many coconut (*phrao*), jackfruit (*lang*), mango (*mak muang*) and tamarind (*mak kham*) plantations" (Penth, 1990) (Figs. 15, 16). This interpretation of the inscription is kindly supplied by Dr Hans Penth, Archive of Lan Na Inscriptions, Social Research Institute, Chiang Mai University. The early date of this inscription, usually taken to be AD 1292, has recently been questioned by some scholars, who propose dates as late as the middle of the nineteenth century (Penth, 1989).

From inscriptions in *wats* (monasteries) within the kingdom of Lan Na, of which Chiang Mai was part for more than two centuries, there are similar indications that areca nuts (and *miang*, see Chapter 11) were current and important items for the chewing habits in Lan Na. From the year AD 1411 inscriptions tell us that after Wat Phra Suwanna Maha Wihan had been built, the king of Chiang Mai and the queen mother donated to its principal Buddha image (as a permanent source of income and / or for consumption in the monastery) paddy fields, villages and a plantation of 10,000 areca trees (*mak . . . dai mün lan*). The governor of Ban Oi in the province of Chiang Rai (AD 1479) donated paddy fields for the upkeep of the Buddha image and inhabitants of Wat Ban Yang Mak Muang. He further donated to the monastery areca (*mak*) in this village with a value of 4,000 cowries (Penth,1990).

At the end of the thirteenth century one of King Rama Khamhaeng's men by the name of Phra Ruang was sent to Sukothai's twin city Sawankhalok to check the state of maintenance of the city temples (Kohnen, 1982). Phra Ruang reported back that the temples and monasteries were in a state of decay. The ceramic roof tiles of the temples were defective or non-existent and the monks needed everyday utensils. Consequently, the king asked Phra Ruang to visit the Yüan court of the Chinese emperor in Peking. He brought back to Thailand a large number of Chinese potters and great amounts of equipment sufficient for setting up kilns at Sukothai and on the Yom river at Sawankhalok about sixty miles to the north. Later, in the year AD 1300, the king himself visited Peking where he is said to have married a Chinese princess and to have brought back with him a number of Chinese potters, who established the kilns of Sukothai (le May, 1954). During the *kathin* ceremony (offering of robes to the monks), which lasted for months during the Sukothai period, there were offerings of piles of areca nuts, piles of flowers and cushions and pillows (Conklin, 1988a).

The celadon ceramic ware of Sawankhalok provides useful archaeological evidence of customs and trade in this period. This celadon, which is characterised by its translucent, watery greyish-green glaze seems—compared with the Sukothai ware—to represent the work of more accomplished craftsmen. The ceramics obviously became very popular and were exported to Indonesia, Japan and the Philippine islands in large quantities. Among the Sawankhalok ceramics produced during the fourteenth and fifteenth centuries are maternity figurines (10–

Fig. 15: Stele of Rama Khamhaeng in the National Museum, Bangkok. The inscription, which is dated around 1300, makes the first mention of areca palm and betel vine plantations in Thailand.

Fig. 16: Stamp issued in 1983 in commemoration of the seventh centenary of the Thai alphabet as used on the stele of Rama Khamhaeng.

15 cm tall) made to meet the practical needs of ritual and magic. Interestingly, some of the heads of these statuettes (almost all figurines are decapitated, thus transferring to the ceramic effigy any childbirth dangers which might have befallen the pregnant woman) show the presence of a lump or swelling of the left cheek (Figs. 17, 18). This lump is believed to represent a bolus, or quid, of betel, being held between the teeth and the inside of the cheek.

One of the earliest accounts of areca nut chewing in Siam[1] was given by the seventeenth-century French ambassador to Siam, M. le Chevalier de Chaumont. In his small descriptive book of 1686 he vividly describes the habit of areca nut chewing, saying (p. 108) that the Siamese love the areca nut above anything else and that they chew it constantly (Fig. 19). L'Abbé de Choisy in his *Journal du voyage de Siam* (1685–6) confirmed this observation: "Main pardessus tout les fruits, les Siamois estiment l'aréque, & le bétel avec la chaux, & ne peuvent pas s'en passer."

At the same time—in 1687—another Frenchman, Simon de la Loubère, visited Siam appointed by King Louis XIV as an extraordinary envoy with full powers for the conclusion of a commercial treaty. Although de la Loubère only stayed in Siam for three months he wrote a book (*Du royaume de Siam*) in two volumes which is universally regarded as the finest work on seventeenth-century Siam. The book, published in 1691 (and the English translation in 1693), contains a wealth of detailed information on almost all aspects of Siamese society. His careful observations are clearly demonstrated in his account, *The Areca and Betel*:

> The *Areca*, which the *Siameses* do call *Plou*, is a kind of great Acorn, which yet wants that wooden Cup wherein our Acorn grows: When this Fruit is yet tender, it has at the center or heart a greyish substance, which is as soft as Pap. As it drys it waxes yellower and harder, and the soft substance it has at the heart grows hard too: It is always very bitter and savory. After having cut it into four parts with a Knife, they take a piece every time, and chew it with a Leaf resembling Ivy called *Betel* by the *Europeans* which are at the *Indies*, and *Mak* by the *Siameses*. They wrap it up to put it the more easily into the mouth, and do put on each a small quantity of Lime made of Cockle-shells, and redded by I know not what art. For this reason the *Indians* do always carry this sort of Lime in a very little China dish, for they put so little on every Leaf, that they consume not much in a day, altho they incessantly make use of the *Areca*, and the *Betel*. The *Areca* whilst-tender wholly consumes in the Mouth, but the dry always leaves some remains. The sensible effect of this Acorn and this Leaf is to excite much spitting, if they care not to swallow the Juice; but it is good to spit out the two or three first Mouthfuls at least, to avoid swallowing the Lime. The other less sensible effects, but which are not doubted in the *Indies*, are to carry from the Gums, perhaps by reason of the Lime, whatever may prejudice them, and to sortifie the Stomach, either by reason of the Juice that swallowed at pleasure, and which may have this quality, or by reason of the superfluous moistures which they discharge by spitting. Thus have I never found any person at *Siam* with a stinking breath, which may be an effect of their natural Sobriety.
>
> Now as the *Areca* and *Betel* do cause a red spittle independently of the red Lime which is mix'd therewith, so they leave a Vermilion Tincture on the Lips and Teeth. It passes over the lips, but by little and little it thickens on the Teeth till they become black: So that persons that delight in neatness, do blacken their Teeth, by reason that otherwise the spittle of the *Areca* and *Betel*, mix'd with the natural whiteness of the Teeth, causes an unpleasant effect, which is remarked in the

---

[1] The name Siam was used until 1939, when it was changed, by order of the Government, to Thailand. In this book the name Siam is used in reference to the historical period when it was in use.

Fig. 17: Sawankhalok celadon figurine depicting a young couple with a newborn child. Both man and woman have a lump in their left cheek, most likely caused by a betel quid. H.: 8.5, d.: 5.2 (Sawankhalok, Central Thailand, fourteenth to sixteenth century).

Fig. 18: Heads of maternity figurines of celadon. The crudely made figurines were most probably used to ward off evil spirits. Some of the figurines, as with the ones shown, reveal a lump in their cheek which is interpreted as a betel bolus. Characteristic green celadon glaze of Sawankhalok (from left to right: h.: 3.4; h.: 3.2 and h.: 3.3) (Sawankhalok, Central Thailand, fourteenth to sixteenth century).

Fig. 19: Title page and p. 108 of le Chevalier de Chaumont's account of Siam published in 1686. The author, the French ambassador to Siam, mentions the habit of betel quid chewing in this early text (see lower part of p. 108).

Fig. 20: (opposite, above) Wihan of Wat Phra Singh, Chiang Mai, where sixteenth-century murals have been preserved. Figure 21 shows a detail of this mural.

Fig. 21: (opposite, below) Mural from Wat Phra Singh, Chiang Mai, Thailand. Detail showing the offering of betel quids to guests.

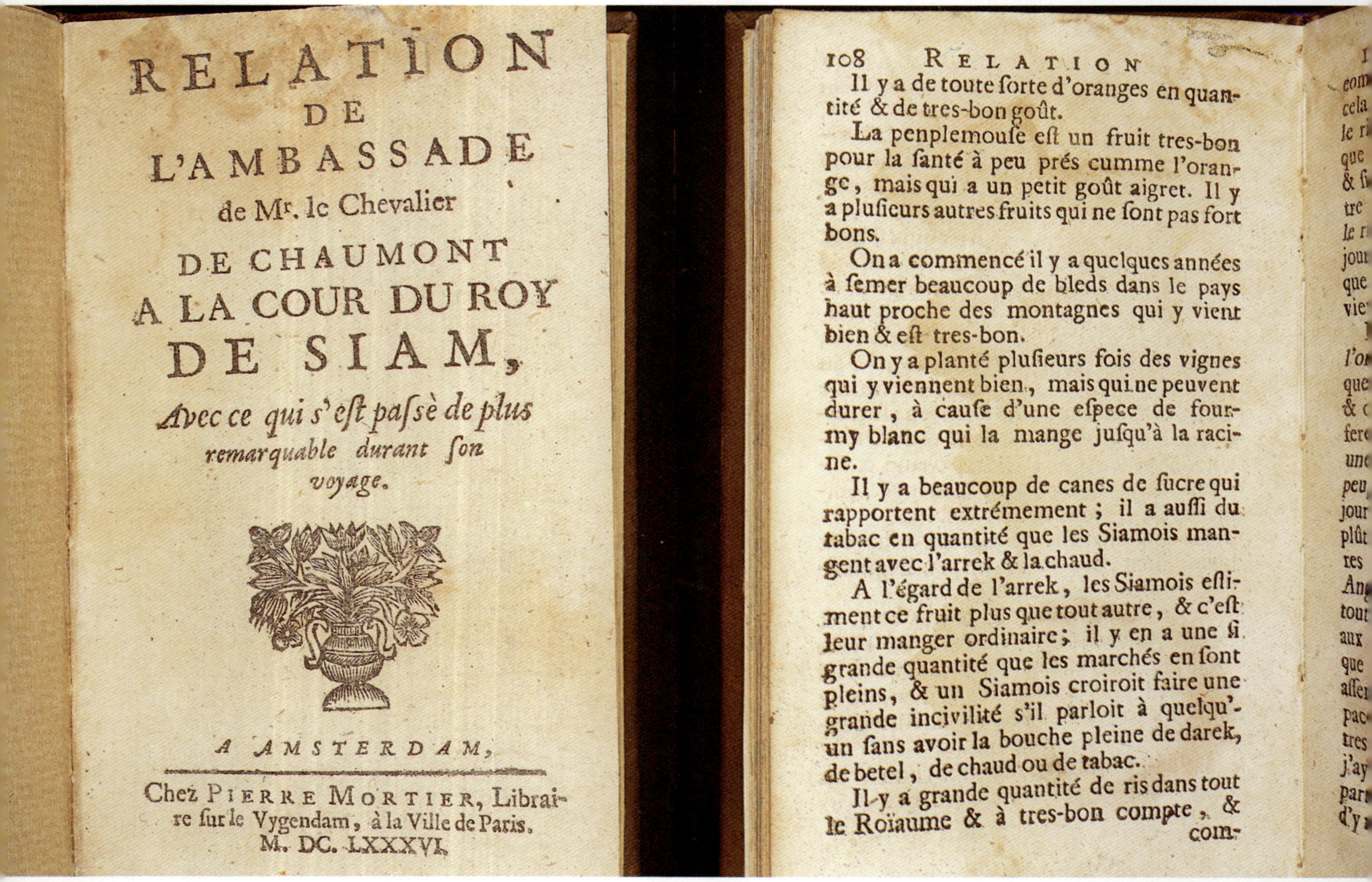

RELATION
DE
L'AMBASSADE
de Mr. le Chevalier
DE CHAUMONT
A LA COUR DU ROY
DE SIAM,
Avec ce qui s'est passé de plus remarquable durant son voyage.

A AMSTERDAM,
Chez PIERRE MORTIER, Libraire sur le Vygendam, à la Ville de Paris.
M. DC. LXXXVI.

108 RELATION

Il y a de toute sorte d'oranges en quantité & de tres-bon goût.

La penplemouse est un fruit tres-bon pour la santé à peu prés cumme l'orange, mais qui a un petit goût aigret. Il y a plusieurs autres fruits qui ne sont pas fort bons.

On a commencé il y a quelques années à semer beaucoup de bleds dans le pays haut proche des montagnes qui y vient bien & est tres-bon.

On y a planté plusieurs fois des vignes qui y viennent bien, mais qui ne peuvent durer, à cause d'une espece de fourmy blanc qui la mange jusqu'à la racine.

Il y a beaucoup de canes de sucre qui rapportent extrémement ; il a aussi du tabac en quantité que les Siamois mangent avec l'arrek & la chaud.

A l'égard de l'arrek, les Siamois estiment ce fruit plus que tout autre, & c'est leur manger ordinaire; il y en a une si grande quantité que les marchés en sont pleins, & un Siamois croiroit faire une grande incivilité s'il parloit à quelqu'un sans avoir la bouche pleine de darek, de betel, de chaud ou de tabac.

Il y a grande quantité de ris dans tout le Roïaume & à tres-bon compte, & com-

common people. I shall transiently declare, that the Vermilion Lips which the *Siameses* saw in the Pictures of our Ladies which we had carried to this Country, made them to say that we must needs have in France, better *Betel* than theirs.

To blacken their Teeth, they do thereon put some pieces of very sowre Lemon, which they hold on their Jaws or Lips for an hour, or more. They report that this softens the Teeth a little. They afterwards rub them with a Juice, which proceeds either from a certain Root, or from the *Coco,* when they are burnt, and so the operation is perform'd. Yet it pleases them sometimes to relate that it continues three days, during which it is necessary, they say, to lye on their Belly and eat no solid Food: But some have assur'd me that this is not true, and that it is sufficient to eat nothing hot for two or three days. I believe rather that their Teeth are too much set on edge, to be able for some time to eat any thing solid. It is necessary continually to renew this operation to make the effect thereof continue; for this Blackness sticks not so strong to the Teeth, but that it may be rub'd off with a burnt Crust of Bread reduc'd to Powder. They love also to redden the Nails of their little Fingers, and for this end they scrape them, and then apply a certain Juice, which they extract from a little Rice bruised in Çitron Juice with some leaves of aree, which in every thing resembles the Pomegranate Tree, but bears no Fruit.

In brief, the *Arequier* or *Arectree,* and all the Trees which are called *Palmites,* have no Branches, but great, long and broad Leaves, like the Palm-tree; and they have their Leaves only at the top of the stalk, which is hollow. These sorts of Trees do annually produce a new Shoot of Leaves, which spring out of the middle of the Leaves of the preceeding year, which then fall off, and leave a mark round the Trunk; so that by these marks which are so many knots, and which are close together, they can easily compute the Years, or Age of the Tree.

Of particular interest also are descriptions of the habit of betel quid chewing from the classical Thai literature which has occasionally been translated into German, English or French. The rowing songs (*Die Ruderlieder; kap he rüö,* Wenk, 1968) from the period of King Rama II contain several verses where betel and its use are described. In the German translation (Wenk, 1968: p. 130) the following verse is included:

> Kap, Betel hast du bereitet, fein und geschickt, das Blatt verlängert, wie liebenswert von dir. Kardamom hinzugetan und Nelken, Tabak, (dies alles), daß ich mich freue.

In another study of Thai literature, Wenk (1982) cites numerous descriptions of the betel habit. One example on p. 121 which includes verses 369 to 380 in German translation is as follows:

> Daher lenkt er sich ab, betrachtet das Ufer, sieht überall Gärten und die vielen, hohen Betelpalmen. Die Früchte der Bäume beugen sich herab bis zu den hervorgewölbten Wurzeln, unreife als auch reife Früchte hängen in Massen herab. Der Betel aus diesem Bezirk Bang Lang ist bekannt. Man nennt diese Art den präparierten Betel. Die Geliebte schnitt (die Früchte) auf, bereitete (mir den Betel), wählte auch, sehr oft, (die Früchte) aus. Ach, nicht einmal diesen Betel, den ich kaute, habe ich jetzt, obwohl der Mund ausgetrocknet ist bis ins Innerste. Fern von der Geliebten muß ich sein. Wer (sonst) kann solchen (Betel) zubereiten!

The popular Thai poem "Khun Chang, Khun Phèn", which was translated by Mme J. Kasem Sibunruang in 1960 (*La femme, le héros et le vilain*) mentions the betel habit several times. One such example (p.23) is:

Lorsque Thong Prasi est d'accord avec son fils,
Elle s'agite et ordonne aux esclaves
De tout préparer pour l'ordination.
Les unes font des krué. . .
Les autres épluchent des noix d'arec;
Ceux-ci roulent des feuilles de bétel,
Ceux-là fabriquent des cierges.

Another example is given on p. 151 where the rite of *yok khân khao* is described:

> A l'arrivée da la sage-femme, *mo tan yé* (terme péjoratif de nos jours), on place sur la table, au milieu de la maison, un bol de riz, *tang khân khao*, sur lequel sont placés: 3 noix d'arec, 21 feuilles de bétel, une dizaine de bananes, 2 cierges et 2 bâtons d'encens avec une petite somme d'argent. Après trois jours d'exposition, on donne ce bol à l'accoucheuse. Cet acte est appelé: *yok khân khao*.

The abundance of literary references to the habit of betel quid chewing is in marked contrast to the relative paucity of depictions of the habit and its characteristic utensils in Thai paintings. One notable exception, however, is the offering of betel to be found on the frescoes representing episodes from the Ramakien, in Wat Phra Keo in Bangkok. These famous frescoes were painted in the reign of King Rama III (1824 to 1850) and were restored several times so that the frescoes which are to be seen today in reality date from 1932. Another well-known scene of offering of betel quid may be seen in the chapel of Wat Phra Singh, Chiang Mai (Fig. 20). These frescoes date back to the sixteenth century and one (Fig. 21) shows the offering of betel quid to the guests of the court.

Fig. 21.1: Areca catechu palm as published in Horti malabarici pars prima, de varii generis Arboribus et fructibus siliquosis, *van Rhede tot Draekestein, H., Amsterdam, 1686.*

Fig. 21.2: Areca catechu with flowers, fruit and areca nut as shown in Getreue Darstellung und Beschreibung der Arzneykunde gebräuchlichen Gewächse, wie auch solcher, welche mit Ihnen verwechselt werden können, *Heyne, F. G., Vol. VII, Berlin, 1821, p. 35*

6. The Habit in Siam During the Nineteenth and Twentieth Centuries

Being such a prevalent habit and an integral part of everyday life among the Thai people, betel chewing and its socio-ritual aspects are often described and commented on in the literature. Finlayson, in his book, *The Mission to Siam, and Hué, the Capital of Cochin China, In the Years 1821–2,* mentioned the betel chewing habit during a royal audience (p. 148): "While these questions were passing, betel was introduced in handsome silver vessels and gold cups." Early in the reign of King Mongkut (1851–1868) the British Government appointed and empowered Sir John Bowring, Governor of Hong Kong, to make a new treaty of commerce with Siam. Based on the year of the mission (1855) Sir John wrote a two-volume book: *The Kingdom and People of Siam* (1857). In the chapter on manners and customs he makes several references to the habit of betel chewing.

> A nobleman never moves about without the bearer of his areca-box, called a *xrob*. Some of these are of solid gold, ornamented with jewels, and are among the customary presents of the King to the higher nobles. When a Siamese sits down, the xrob-bearer deposits the box on the ground, so near that his master can conveniently reach it. It is in constant requisition. The consumption of the areca and the betel nut is enormous throughout Siam. A Siamese who is tolerably well off is scarcely ever seen without the nut in his mouth; and he is invariably attended by servants who carry a supply of the material, with all the needful paraphernalia, whose costliness depends upon the opulence and rank of the possessor. Among the nobles the boxes are almost invariably of gold; and in the case of the very highest ranks, they are covered with diamonds or other precious stones, and are constantly in a state of passage from the hands of the servants to their masters, and back again when the want of the moment has been supplied. These boxes hold the fresh leaves of the betel, the areca-nut, and the pink chunam, or quicklime coloured with curcuma. The chewing of areca produces a large quantity of blood-coloured saliva, which is spit into spittoons of earthenware, brass, silver, or gold, according to the rank of the party. Betel-chewing blackens the teeth, which is considered a recommendation in Siam; it purifies the breath, and is said to be a preservative of the tooth's enamel when used moderately and without a undue quantity of quicklime. The betel is such a necessary of life in Siam, that were the choice offered to a hungry Siamese of food, or his favourite betel, there is no doubt he would reject the first, and ask for the second in preference.

Like Sir John Bowring a multitude of Western travellers and envoys visiting Siam during the nineteenth century and the first half of the twentieth century have been fascinated—or repelled—by the ubiquitous habit of betel chewing so strange to European eyes.

F. A. Neale, formerly in the service of the Siamese Royalty wrote in 1852 the following—not very flattering—account on the Siamese female:

> The Siamese ladies may without the smallest fear of competition proclaim themselves to be *the* ugliest race of females upon the face of the globe. As though nature had not formed them sufficiently ugly, these most neglected of all the human species, resort to dyes wherewith to dye their teeth and lips a jet black colour. The darker the teeth the more beautiful is a Siamese belle considered; and in order that their gums should be of a brilliant red to form a pleasant contrast to the black lips and teeth, they resort to the pleasant pastime of chewing *betel* from morning till night.

And Neale goes on to describe the traditional ingredients of the betel quid. Neale's vivid description of the habit, which in the preface to his book is characterised as at best semi-barbarous, ends:

> As they never swallow the juice the results are very detrimental to the cleanliness of the floors of the houses and of themselves generally. They commonly make use of two such quids during the day and this horrid mixture has the effect of dyeing their gums and the whole of the palate and tongue a blood red colour.

Another resident who had reservations about the habit was Miss M. L. Cort, a missionary to Siam during the last century.

Conklin (1988a) wrote that: "The Siamese kiss with their noses by pressing them against their friend's and saying 'fragrant, very fragrant' . . . while they take long satisfied sniffs. Many are now learning to shake hands and make graceful bows like Europeans but the imported kiss is not yet in vogue and I do not see that it ever can be until betel is discarded, for at the present the nose is a more kissable feature of the Siamese face than the mouth."

In the middle and second half of the nineteenth century Malcolm Smith was physician to the Court of Siam—for five years in an official capacity and for many more years unofficially. He wrote (1947) a colourful description of his life as a court physician. Not surprisingly this includes an account on the betel quid chewing habit:

> The habit of chewing betel-nut was in those days universal, both by men and women. Many of them chewed it continually the only interruption being for their meals. The rich were never without their betel-box and its necessary companion the spittoon, which was carried by servants who walked behind them. Many of these boxes were ornamented with precious stones, and it was possible to gauge the rank of a person by value of his box. To receive one from the king or queen was a great honour. The constant chewing of the nut stained the teeth black, and thus it came about that what was once the result of a habit developed into a fashion. The women of Siam who took pride in their personal appearance were not satisfied with just black teeth, they must be shining black. Any defective spots were touched up with a black pigment which always formed part of the toilet outfit.

Carl Bock, who travelled in Siam during the years 1881–82 gives in his book *Temples and Elephants* (1884) several vivid accounts of the habit. He points out that the areca nut—as in India—plays a conspicuous part in the wedding ceremony:

> It is a curious fact that which gives the name to the whole wedding-ceremony is the betel-nut which is served on the occasion on a metal or plaited tray. This article in order to be complete must have three accompaniments, viz. a cake, called Kanom-cheen; a kind of mincemeat, highly seasoned, wrapped in plantain-leaves, and, cooked by steaming; and thirdly, the sirih-leaf and red lime. These are all termed Kan mak, literally, a basin of betel-nut, and this is the common Siamese name for a wedding.

From his visit to Lao-land (Northern Siam) Bock gives this portrayal of toothless betel chewers:

> Teeth or no teeth, every Laosian, from almost infancy to old age, chews betel. The toothless old folks assist nature by placing the betel-nut with the accompanying ingredients into a small mortar—a sort of hybrid between a child's popgun and a syringe, which they always carry with them; a few strokes of the rod suffice to crush the nuts and reduce them to a pulpy mass warranted not to hurt the softest gums.

Bock's personal view on the habits of chewing and smoking is clearly expressed:

> This perpetual cramming of the mouth with betel is not conducive to ease in conversation, and the Laosians seem to seize on every occasion for conversation as an opportunity for replenishing the mouth. The habit is very unpleasant, owing to the blackness which it imparts to the teeth as much as to the incessant spitting it gives rise to, and to the necessity for ever and anon removing the re-

mains of the quid from the mouth. It is said to assist digestion: but it seems to me to corrode and rot the teeth. Tobacco is smoked, not only by men, but by women and children. How the men find time to smoke between the intervals of betel-chewing, and how they find time to chew between the intervals of smoking, it is hard to say.

It has been said that around the mid-nineteenth century noble gentlemen living in Bangkok possessed two sets of false teeth. When attending a Thai function they wore the blackstained set (stained through the use of betel quids) whereas the set carrying non-stained, white teeth was used when a European party was thrown.

Maxwell Sommerville (Conklin, 1988a), a visiting professor from the University of Pennsylvania made this charming observation of a Bangkok market in 1897:

> The most frequent or common occupation is the business of preparing the betel-nut for chewers; every little distance one goes through the bazaar—in fact, throughout the city—petty merchants who support themselves by pandering to that pernicious habit may be seen preparing the betel-nut for the ordinary people . . . . The dealers cut up their green leaves into the proper triangular form, crack the nuts, and with wooden spatulas work the turmeric-stained lime into a paste. It is amusing to see how skilfully they form the pieces of green leaf into pointed, cone-shaped cups, into each one of which they place a portion of the ingredients.

As a supplement to the above we may quote from the anonymous article entitled "The Betel Tree", originally published in the little-known *Bangkok Calendar for 1864*:

> The natives of Siam much prefer the nut in a fresh state, before it is fully ripe. For this purpose, they first divide the entire fruit, with its hull, into longitudinal quarters, and then cleave each quarter of the nut from its covering, by means of a slender knife, cutting (native fashion) outward from the thumb and fingers which hold it—very dexterously managing to leave a small bit of the inner and lower part of the hull on each quarter, to serve as a delicate handle, by which it can be the more gracefully put into the mouth. The work of thus preparing the Betel-nut for chewing, falls by custom exclusively upon the women and girls, in which they spend a large portion of their time. To have it thus made ready, is a mark of politeness always due from them to the males, more especially their own relatives and friends, and to all whom they wish to make their friends. Wives must prepare it for their husbands, sisters for their brothers and sweet-hearts for their lovers. But if the nut be in a dried state, the work seems by common consent to fall into the hands of the more muscular sex. They break it up into a fine powder in a metallic barrel as large as the lower end of a common musket, and about eight inches long, open at each end, one end being smaller than the other. Putting a wooden plug into the small extremity, they drive the nut down from the other end upon it, and there break it to pieces, with a gouge-like pestle neatly fitted in a spheroid handle, generally made of ivory.
>
> The nut when thus broken into small particles, and commingled with vermilion coloured lime-paste and a little cerileaf, is then driven out of the mortar, plug and all, by the way it was driven in, and forms a delicious mouthful, or cud, for the aged and toothless. Indeed all classes are sometimes reduced to the necessity of preparing their Betel-nut in this way at certain seasons, when the fresh nut cannot readily be obtained.

After describing the effects of chewing on the saliva, lips and teeth the writer concludes with an interesting description of the vermilion-coloured lime paste mentioned above.

> This (the plastic lime) is made of newly burnt stone lime. Before the burnt stone has been slaked, an infusion of turmeric root is poured upon it, which causes it to fall into powder taking a fine vermilion color. Enough of the infusion is employed

to leave the lime in a plastic state. In this state it is brought to market, sometimes in large masses of several hundred weight, ready to be laded out into little earthen pots, holding less than half a pint each. These little vessels accompany the pedlar, and he will commonly sell twenty of them for seven and a half cents, or a bucket full containing three gallons, for fifteen cents.

This plastic lime is spread on each cerileaf with a wooden spatula as we spread butter on bread; and then rolling the leaf up with the *lime-butter* inside, it is immediately put into the mouth to join the Betel already in the mill. Not satisfied with this, the natives (more especially the women) will take up a pinch of cut tobacco and hold it deliciously between the upper front teeth and the lip. But it should be said that Siamese women seldom smoke tobacco, while the males are the most inveterate smokers, even from infancy, before they have been weaned from their mother's breast.

An amusing story is told by Wood (1965) in his book *Consul in Paradise*, where he refers to what are good and bad manners, particularly in relation to the Thais' habit of spitting:

For instance, English and American people of the more cultured classes rather dislike spitting in public, but in Siam there is not much prejudice against this habit. Until comparatively recent times, the chewing of betel-nut was very widely indulged in, and this rendered it necessary for people to keep on spitting at very frequent intervals. Spittoons were among the most prominent household utensils, and a gold spittoon even formed part of the regalia of Siam. If you paid a visit to an old-fashioned Siamese house, a spittoon of generous proportions was usually placed beside you as soon as you sat down; sometimes two were provided, or even three—one on each side, and a small one on the table for use in emergency. Chewing is not a common habit now, and the cultivation of the betel-nut—or, more correctly, the areca nut—is only carried on in a small way. Siamese and Lao of the younger generation usually have the most beautiful white teeth, but when I first came to the country white teeth were so rare as to be looked upon as an eccentricity; to foreigners those black mouths appeared repulsive, but the Siamese did not regard them as a disfigurement. In former times, when I was entertaining Siamese guests of old-fashioned tastes, who did not like to go too long without their betel-nut, I always had a supply ready for them. On one occasion I had prepared a beautiful chewing outfit, spittoon included, and had told my servant, a new and raw lad, that he would find the betel-tray and the spittoon in the bedroom, and that he must bring them into the drawing-room and place them near our distinguished Siamese guest as soon as we had finished dinner. When the time came, the boy brought along the betel-tray all right, but instead of the spittoon he imported from the bedroom a utensil of an altogether different sort, not usually seen in drawing-rooms, and plonked it down boldly in the midst of the assembled company. Some of the ladies eyed it askance, but I thought it best to make light of the matter, so I merely remarked: Not that one, boy, please. The other one—without a handle.

7. Betel Quid Ingredients and Their Production in Thailand

As in all betel chewing societies a number of variations in the chewing habit are also found in Thailand. However, the basic components of the betel quid are the same throughout the country. The areca nut, though prepared in different ways, is always used together with the betel leaf, either fresh or fermented, and with lime, which is usually white or pink. Tobacco is commonly used in all provinces of Thailand as part of the betel quid. In Figures 22 to 26 the different constituents of the betel quid as used in Northern Thailand are shown. Catechu or *sisiat* is often added to the quid and in Northern Thailand the *goh* bark is a popular ingredient. The latter is the bark of an oak tree of which two varieties are known, *goh lek and goh paen* (Q. semiserrata Roxb.; Castanoposis diversifolia King).The bark has a red-brownish colour and an astringent taste (Figs. 23, 24, 26).

It is of interest to note that the betel chewing hill tribes, particularly the Karen, Akha, Lisu and Lahu normally do not use *sisiat* or *goh* bark because these are not readily available.

In Southern Thailand, in addition to the basic components of the betel quid, a specific type of soil called *mid* in Southern Thai, which is found in the Hat Yai area is used (Fig. 27). In this part of Thailand cooked areca nuts are available on the market (*mak dam* or *mak dong*) (Figs. 28, 29) and it is said that these are for elderly people who prefer areca nuts in this form because they are softer and thus easier to chew than the fresh nut.

The agricultural significance of the areca nut

While the origin of the Areca catechu L. palm tree is still debated, its wild variety was described as early as 1623 as *pinlang*, a term still used today for the areca nut in Malaysia and Sumatra. It was long suggested that the areca palm had its origin in this particular area. However, no wild areca palm trees are found here to support this suggestion. Wild areca palms are found in the Philippines and in Sri Lanka but again, evidence for its origin there is uncertain. As mentioned earlier, there is evidence that areca palm trees have been present in Thailand for at least 700 years. In colloquial Thai people usually talk of *mak phlu*, meaning both ingredients of the betel quid, namely the areca nut and the betel leaves.

The areca palm is found and is still cultivated in almost every part of Thailand. Areca palms grow in small groups in individual gardens or in large plantations, particularly in the southern parts of the country. In the suburbs of Bangkok, the palm was once grown in gardens in orderly rows. During the Krung Thonburi and Rattanakosin period, up to the beginning of the twentieth century, owners of areca palm trees had to pay tax on the production of areca nuts. During the years 1882–1883 no fewer than 7,644,915 areca palms were registered for which tax had to be paid. Graham (1924) in *Siam: Nature and Industry*, wrote of areca nuts (p. 226–27):

There is quite a large area planted with areca, but no official figures of its extent are available. Nearly every peasant grows a few areca-palms, if his soil is at all suitable, but these are simply for his own use. In some districts, however, the areca is grown for the market. There are large plantations in Chumpawn, Langsuan, Surat, Patalung, Nakon Sritamarat and other provinces.

Plantation areas were formerly found in Thonburi and Nonthaburi province. Here the *mak bang bon* was produced but it was not very popular among the people because of its unpleasant taste when chewed together with the leaves. Obviously, three kinds of *mak bang bon* were available: a reddish sweet *mak*, the really sweet *mak* and the astringent sweet *mak*. The *bang lang* area

Fig. 22: Betel stall in Central Lamjai Market, Chiang Mai (1990). From left to right: Dried sliced areca nuts, fresh areca fruits and betel leaves. Pink and white lime. Small packages of ready-made betel quids with the major components.

Fig. 23: Betel stall in a market at Mae Rim (Chiang Mai province, 1990). From left to right: In the left corner bags with tobacco. Catechu. Strings of sliced areca nuts. Goh bark in bundles in red plastic container. White and pink lime in small plastic bags. Slightly fermented betel leaves in bundles in blue plastic container. Sliced and sun-dried areca nuts. The shallow greenish bowl contains a string of areca nuts and some catechu.

Fig. 24 (overleaf, above): Ready-made betel quids and some ingredients from Lamjai Market, Chiang Mai, 1990. Several fresh betel leaves (centre) are rolled in the form of a horn containing pink lime. To the right are the reddish-brown goh bark and the orange-segment-shaped areca nuts on a string. To the left is tobacco wrapped in a banana leaf.

Fig. 25 (overleaf, below): Close-up of a betel leaf which has been prepared with pink lime. The rolled-up leaf contains pieces of the areca nut, tobacco and cutch.

Fig. 26: Betel set of lacquer and wooden boxes showing the main ingredients as used in Northern Thailand. The three wooden boxes contain, from left to right: Tobacco, reddish goh bark and catechu (Chiang Mai, Thailand, 1990).

Fig. 27: Main components of the betel quid as used on the island of Phuket, Thailand (1990). Besides the betel leaf and areca nut, red lime and tobacco are used. The two yellowish-brown pieces in the lower left corner represent a particular type of soil (mid) found in Hat Yai, which is chewed with the betel quid.

Fig. 28: Cooked areca fruits. This variety is used in Southern Thailand by elderly people in place of the very hard dried or fresh areca nut (Phuket, Southern Thailand, 1990).

Fig. 29: A cooked areca nut has been opened to demonstrate the husk and shows some delicate brown-orange patterns characteristic of areca nuts.

Fig. 30 (opposite, above): Areca fruits of different varieties and stages of ripeness. The pointed drop-like red variety is rare in Northern Thailand (Chiang Mai, Thailand).

Fig. 31 (opposite, below): Ovoid areca fruits with orange husk, one cut open to reveal the characteristic silvery-white nut with irradiating fibres (Phuket, Thailand).

Fig. 32 (overleaf, top left): Areca nuts are split open using knives. In the small factories of Northern Thailand it is usually women who perform this kind of tedious work (Chiang Mai, Thailand).

Fig. 33 (overleaf, top right): Sliced areca nuts set out for drying in the sun (Sansai district, Chiang Mai province, Thailand).

Fig. 34 (overfleaf, bottom right): Bundles of stringed areca nuts and husk cut in the form of an orange segment (Sansai district, Chiang Mai province, Thailand).

Fig. 35 (overleaf, bottom left): Close-up of sun-dried areca nuts on a bamboo string as sold in Northern Thai markets (Central Market, Chiang Mai, Thailand).

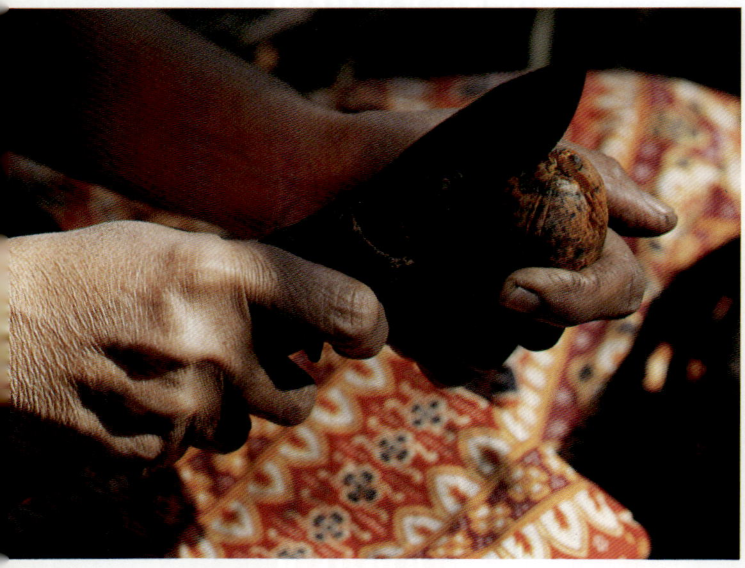

of Bangkok Noi and Rachaburana in Thonburi province as well as Phrapadaeng in Samut Prakan province produced *mak bang lang* which was said to be the best of all areca nuts. *Mak bang lang* was introduced into several other provinces such as Chantaburi and Nakhon Pathom. Today the largest plantation areas are found in Chachoengsao (12,637 rai; one rai = 0.395 acres). In most other provinces of Thailand areca palms are only found in home gardens.

The process of drying areca nuts

Several botanical species of areca nuts are known. In the northern part of Thailand the *mak prao* is said to be rare while the *mak muang* is the more common type (Figs. 30, 31). The round areca nuts usually are larger and have a uniformly thick husk compared to the tapered variety. According to the stage of ripeness and species areca nuts appear as light greenish, golden, yellow, orange and red. While areca nuts, particularly in the southern part of Thailand may be harvested throughout the year, they are best harvested during the months of March to May and August to September. The harvesting is done by men who climb up the areca palm trees. They use a knife to cut the stem of the bundle of areca nuts and the bundle of nuts falls down to the ditch surrounding the palm trees. The nuts may also be brought down by hand or be harvested by using a special instrument consisting of a sharp knife or hook at the end of a long pole of bamboo. After harvesting the areca nuts are taken to the market and sold there in their fresh state. Alternatively, they are prepared in different ways prior to being sold. A common way of preparing the areca nut is by slicing (Fig. 32). The product is called *mak soi*. After removal of the husk the nut is cut into two pieces and slices of 3–4 mm thickness are prepared. These are kept in the sunlight for two to three days for drying (Fig. 33). One worker is said to be able to slice about 900 to 1,000 areca nuts per day.

Cutting the areca nut into segments resembling orange slices (*mak clip som*) is another variety of preparation. One nut can be cut into four to five pieces, depending on the size. The process of sun-drying takes two to five days. *Mak jian* or *mak siao* is another variety where the whole nut including the husk is cut into four to five pieces. In the northern province of Chiang Mai these pieces are often mounted on strings of bamboo, dried and sold in this form in the markets (Figs. 34, 35). Naturally, the whole nuts may also be dried with or without the husk. Many other minor modifications in the preparation are known, a fact which is expressed nicely in the variety of terms for these products: *mak van, mak-e-pae, mak hun, mak pon, mak-pa-song, mak-pa-seek, mak-pa-see* or *mak guk*. About 1,000 areca nuts of the fresh or raw variety make up three to four kilograms of dried *mak*. Chewers usually purchase at one time sufficient areca nut and quid ingredients for one or two days' consumption.

Remarks on the marketing of areca nuts

Areca nuts were an important trading commodity in Thailand before 1932 when the Government discouraged the habit of betel chewing. In 1982 the areca nut became an important economic commodity again. In the year 1985, 23,494 tons, with a value of 480 million Baht, were exported. Countries other than Thailand which export areca nuts include Burma, Sri Lanka, Malaysia, Indonesia and the Philippines. Countries which import areca nuts from Thailand are Pakistan, Malaysia, Bangladesh, Singapore and India. Besides the original use as the main ingredient for the betel quid, areca nuts are also used for industrial purposes, for example as a basic compound of drugs or in bleaching agents for leather dyes. The price of the nut depends on the season as well as on the quality. Prices may range from 10 Baht per 100 nuts in the high season to one areca nut for one to three Baht during the off-season. Generally, the dried variety is more expensive than the fresh areca nut. In 1985 the price in Chachoengsao province for fresh areca nuts was 10 to 12 Baht per 100 nuts and the *mak soi* sliced nuts fetched 25 to 40 Baht per kilogram. In

Nakhon Si Thammarat for the same variety (*mak soi*) the price was 75 Baht per kilogram. While the habit of betel chewing is likely to gradually disappear the slender beautiful palm will still be around since the areca nut has now become an industrial commodity.

Betel leaves

In *Siam, Nature and Industry* published in 1930 by the Ministry of Commerce and Communications, we read:

Of the order *Piperaceae* most of the species are indigenous in Southern Siam on both the east and west sides of the gulf. *Piper Betle* (Siamese *Phlu*) is cultivated extensively in all parts, the leaves being used for chewing with the Areca nut. The plant is a vine, grows best in the shade and requires a good deal of water. The leaves are deep glossy green and have a pleasantly-pungent aromatic taste.

While in the northern parts of Thailand only individual plants are grown in home gardens there are many orchards of betel vine from Bangkok to the southern part of Thailand, particularly in the Nakhon Chaisi district of Nakhon Pathom province. A detailed description of these orchards was published in *Today's Agriculture Magazine* of September 1982. In Nakhon Pathom province there are more than 20 plantations of betel vine, from which the production is sufficient to allow fresh betel leaves to be exported to India, Pakistan and Sri Lanka. Piper betle plants are quite resistant to attacks by insects and may survive under normal conditions for more than 10 years. In Thailand, three different types of fresh betel leaves are known: 1) the China variety, 2) the yellow and 3) the green fresh betel leaf. Leaves are usually plucked early in the morning and transported to markets in a fresh state. As has been stated earlier, a fermented variety of the betel leaf is also known in Thailand. However, this is not as popular as the fresh betel leaf. While in former times huge quantities of fresh betel leaves were to be seen in the markets, nowadays there are only a few stalls to serve the dwindling numbers of betel chewing customers. Betel leaves have lost the significance they once had as a popular commodity.

Other quid ingredients

While lime and catechu have little or no significance economically, tobacco is an important commodity in Thailand. It is, however, quite evident that tobacco is not grown to satisfy the decreasing number of betel quid chewers who add raw tobacco to the quid.

Fig. 35.1: Early print of the areca palm tree published in Voyage de Siam des Pères Jesuites, with the areca fruit as well as the betel vine, Vol. 6, 1687.

Fig. 35.2: The Siamese king: "le Roy monté sur son Elephant" as published by Tachard, Vol. 1.

Fig. 35.3: "A Betel and Pinangh Garden" showing the betel vines on the left and the areca palm trees on the right. Johan Nieuhof, Voyages and Travels to the East Indies, *1653–1670, London, 1704.*

8. The Habit in Thailand Today

In historical documents, books and reports by travellers it has been stated again and again that until the twentieth century betel chewing was extremely widespread in Siam.

De Young (1955) in his studies of village life in Thailand in the early 1950s came to the conclusion that a number of old customs such as the ear piercing ceremony and many other traditions had been given up in rural Northern Thailand. On the habit of betel chewing de Young stated:

> Betel chewing, once a universal custom among Thai peasants is beginning to show signs of decline. Most villagers over the age of 35 still chew betel quids although there are a few exceptions. Below this age very few modern villagers indulge in chewing. The younger villagers today very definitely have been indoctrinated in school against betel chewing, and in all likelihood many of the present school generation will not turn to it.

Observers of Thai life writing 50 years ago all remark on the widespread habit of betel chewing among both young and old, noting that little girls, in particular, began to chew betel quid before their top-knots were cut at the age of 12 or 13.

It would be almost impossible to find a child of this age chewing in rural Thailand today. School and health authorities repudiated the custom, and during World War II, when Field-Marshal Pibulsongkram was prime minister, he tried to abolish it by making it illegal. In the Act of National Culture (1942) it is stated that the Thai people should stop betel quid chewing (Consumption Culture), and it was forbidden to spit saliva and betel fluid on roads and public places (Society Culture). This was part of his overall modernisation drive which also included the use of fork and spoon, rather than the bare hand, for eating, and the compulsory wearing of hats and Western-style trousers and shirt for men instead of the traditional *pa-kao-ma*. Habitual chewers ignored the ministerial decree and finally it was quietly dropped. The Thai peasant of the past had a mouth full of black teeth, and a gleaming white smile in the old days was to a certain extent a mark of depravity. To have black teeth during those times was in fact regarded as an absolute necessity in order to demonstrate the difference between a human being and an animal. Similar beliefs are known from the island of Bali where the ceremony of filing the canine teeth in both boys and girls has a comparable meaning. The tips of the canines are ground so that the wearer cannot in any way be mistaken for a carniverous animal. Also of interest are de Young's comments on the start of the of chewing habit. Peasants say that while there is no particular time for a person to start chewing betel, generally, if he does so, it will be around the age of 30 to 35. This is the period when a woman has had several children in quick succession and when men have been working in the fields for 15 years or more. And Pindborg made this observation in 1973:

> Any visitor to Thailand has noticed the red spittings on the street indicating the wide-spread use of betel. This ghastly sight which indeed is extremely common in large cities of South Asia such as Delhi in India is extremely rare these days in the large cities of Thailand. Indeed, the urban people and particularly the Bangkokians have now after so many centuries almost given up the use of betel quid chewing. Again in contrast to cities in India betel quid stalls which are so common there are hardly ever found on the streets of Bangkok and it is difficult to locate more than one or two stalls even in large markets. When interviewing the market stall owners, mostly old ladies, the answer is always the same, be it in Northern Thailand, in Bangkok or in Southern Thailand: My customers are old ladies and old men who usually buy small quantities every day. Young Thai people never indulge in betel chewing.

In his book *More Thai Ways* (1989) Denis Segaller reports an interview with a confirmed betel quid chewer, a 75-year-old woman from Petchaburi province. Being asked why she chews she answers: "To pass the time, and sweeten the breath. It's also *aroy*—pleasant to the taste—and although you can only chew it little by little, you become addicted, and can't stop." Questioned about the possible removal of the red stain from her teeth she answers: "Yes—we use a special kind of liquid called *ya ploy see* (medicine to remove the colour) and clean the teeth with a dried areca nut husk." She is obviously not hesitant in answering the question as to whether more women than men chew betel quids: "Oh, yes—lots and lots of women!"

While the number of betel chewers in the large cities is steadily decreasing the habit is still quite prevalent in rural areas of Thailand. Epidemiologic studies among rural Northern Thai have shown that betel chewing is still practised but that there were no betel chewers below the age of 50. These studies also revealed that in younger individuals the universal habit of cigarette smoking obviously has taken over. It was also of interest that betel chewing was more common in women than men and that catechu and tobacco were almost always included in the betel quid (Reichart et al., 1987).

Studies based on statistical material from the Medical Faculty, University of Chiang Mai, have recently shown that the frequency of oral cancer in the provinces of Northern Thailand apparently is decreasing (Reichart et al., 1990). While oral cancer has long been one of the most frequent cancers of the body in this geographical region it seems that other forms and types of cancer have now taken over. Numerous factors are likely to be involved in this change but it cannot be ruled out that the decline in the habit of betel chewing is an important contributing factor to this shift in the cancer frequency pattern. The role of areca nut and tobacco chewing in the aetiology of oral cancer is widely accepted. A very recent review on oral cancer in India by Sankaranarayanan (1990) considered the role of areca nut and tobacco as well as other contributing factors for oral cancer. Since betel quid chewing is still a widespread habit in India, in contrast to Thailand, it was suggested in this paper that intervention studies and research for cancer prevention and treatment is necessary. In conclusion, oral cancers induced by betel quid and tobacco chewing are among the very few human cancers for which our understanding of the aetiology has reached a state to allow the formulation of programmes aiming at the reduction and ultimate elimination of morbidity from these cancers.

There is no answer yet to the question of why betel quid chewing is disappearing in urban centres and, with a certain time lag, in rural communities also. There must, however, be a correlation between social status and the decision to give up or continue the habit of betel chewing. This hypothesis is of particular interest in connection with studies of the betel chewing habits of the Northern Thai hill tribes. Betel chewing is not, as might be suspected, prevalent among all hill tribes in the northern part of Thailand. During past centuries six major groups of highland people have settled in the mountains of Northern Thailand, Burma and Laos. The Akha, Karen, Lahu, Lisu, Meo and Yao are of Tibeto-Burman or Jao-Meo-Pateng origin. Most of these peoples have preserved their original way of life and culture, although changes are evident due to contacts with Thai society as well as to tourism. Most of the hill tribes are betel quid chewers to a certain extent. A study of the chewing and smoking habits of the P'wo Karen, a subgroup of the Karen from Amphoe Omkoi district, revealed that 46 per cent of the women and 29 per cent of the men were betel chewers. It was also of interest that among the Karen who are generally considered to be the poorest of the Northern Thai hill tribes, the habit of chewing betel starts at between the ages of 11 and 30. In fact all age groups, and particularly the older people, were betel chewers. Betel chewing was also observed among the Lahu and Lisu. While about 40 per cent of the population in Lahu villages were chewers, only 20 per cent in the Lisu villages reported this habit (Reichart et al., 1987). Akhas are also heavy chewers but no data are available. The chewing of *miang* is another habit of Northern Thailand, Burma and Laos which is still found in rural societies and some hill tribes like the Meo but which is also on the decline. This particular habit was studied among Northern Thai farmers and it was found that the mean age among *miang* chewers was 58.5 years with a range of 21 to 85 years (Reichart et al., 1988). This is another indication that the habit of *miang* chewing will eventually disappear. See further discussion in Chapter 11 below.

If, out of sheer curiosity, you are tempted to chew a quid yourself before the habit vanishes from everyday life, it may be worthwhile to read the following comments and observations made by two Thai people who in 1964 (Tucker, 1984) determined that knowledge of the habit is best gained through the empirical method. With the assistance of Mrs Nom Saowan, daughter of a former governor of Lopburi province, the two test persons sat on a mat for the ritual of the betel quid.

Mrs Nom demonstrated the preparation of the betel in the following steps.

1 Cut the stem of a betel-pepper leaf, then pare with a very fine knife two round slices from the soft part of the leaf.
2. Smear with spatula a small portion of the red lime paste onto a leaf slice and roll it into a tight little cone.
3. Twiddle some cotton wool into a thin thread and tie the leaf cone. Put away into its container.
4. Select one of the green betel nuts. The round ones are preferred to the oval ones because tradition holds that they cause less of the possible dizziness or fainting spells sometimes induced by the toxic ingredients (lemon is the antidote).
5. Carefully scrape away layers of the outer, green rind of the nut so that they form a multiple skirt around base of nut.
6. Cut nut into 8 or 9 wedges and store in container.
7. Smear lips with some of the perfumed, often rouged, pomade from its box to prevent nut acid from stinging too much on lips.
8. Take one of the leaf cones, deftly remove thread, add one of the nut wedges and slowly insert both together into mouth, chewing vigorously to mix the two.

So much for the regular user. The initiate now will experience such an onrush of saliva from the strongly astringent, pungent, and terribly bitter mixture, that he will either eject the entire cud unceremoniously into the ready spittoon, or try to hold it in, swallowing some of the bitter juice regardless of how much he has been warned against it. This trickle of betel juice will keep his gullet and stomach taut for hours—or so it seems.

A second attempt, after a proper interval for recuperation, might turn out more successfully. Prepared for the onrush of saliva and the bitter taste, the novice will hold the cud, work it together gingerly, tears streaming down his cheeks from the effort not to choke, and finally produce, to the applause and delight of his Thai teachers, the first ejection of pink or red juice into the spittoon. He has graduated and may rid his mouth of the whole thing and grab for the thoughtfully provided sweets or beverage.

While the habits of chewing betel and *miang* are likely to disappear completely from rural as well as urban society in Thailand in a few more years, it is likely that their influence on Thai colloquial language may last for many years to come. Thai expressions for hard times or a period of scarcity—*khao yahk, mak paeng*—"rice is hard to find, betel is expensive" or a more lighthearted expression—*jaek mak*, literally to hand out betel—in other words, to punch someone in the mouth and draw blood, producing a red mouth like that of a betel quid chewer, will remain in use. Similarly, it is likely that the use of betel quid ingredients as therapeutics will survive. A recent article (Kumnung, 1987) describes in detail the preparation of medicine from betel leaves, lime and areca nuts for the cure of colds, coughing, constipation, toothache, foul breath (halitosis) and fresh wounds.

Fig. 35.4: Stamp published in 1992 to commemorate the 60th birthday of Her Majesty the Queen showing a royal betel set.

9. Utensils for the Preparation of the Betel Quid

A number of utensils[1] for preparing the betel quid have been developed over hundreds of years for those indulging in this habit.

The hard areca nut—if bought as a whole nut—needs to be cut into small pieces or even ground into powder if the user has few or no teeth. Lime has to be kept in containers so that it does not dry out.

Sets of betel utensils had to be available in order that hosts might offer betel quids to guests and friends. Thus, over the centuries a series of utensils designed for each particular purpose have been produced: betel leaf holders, lime containers with spatulas, areca nut cutters or knives, boxes and betel quid stands. While the utensils are nothing more than specialised instruments there exist considerable differences in their practical value and as regards artistic and aesthetic presentation. Craftsmanship and artistic traditions, as well as the availability of materials, have widely influenced the final presentation of betel quid paraphernalia. Architectural design such as is found in the pagodas or stupas of Thailand, Cambodia, Laos, Vietnam and Burma has influenced the shapes and forms of betel quid paraphernalia, especially the lime containers. Traditional motives and designs of Buddhist iconography or mythology such as dragons, animals of the week, month or year or stylised flowers have been widely used in the decoration of the utensils. The great variety in form, shape and choice of material has been described and illustrated in several articles and monographs (Conklin, 1988a and 1988b; Verwilghen, 1985; Klebert, 1983; Ashabranner, 1982; Chongkol, 1982; Buddle, 1976; Thierry, 1969; Millot, 1965 among others).

Classification of the utensils reveals a certain homogeneity throughout the geographic area where betel chewing is prevalent. The basic categories of accessories used for the preparation of a betel quid include:

Lime containers, mainly pots of different forms. A large variety of materials including silver, bronze, ceramic, wood, bamboo are used for their production.

Spatulas to remove lime from the lime containers and to spread lime onto the betel leaves. The size of spatulas varies considerably as does the material used. Different metals, wood and bamboo are all used.

Areca nut cutters or knives to cut the nut into pieces. While blades are usually made from iron, cutters may be made of bronze, copper, iron or brass, often decorated with silver.

Mortar (pounder) and pestle to crush the areca nut into small pieces or powder. These are mostly cylindrical in form and made of bronze, brass or wood.

Betel leaf holders, cylindrical in form and made of bamboo or in the shape of a horn (horn of plenty) and made of silver, brass or lacquer ware.

Boxes to contain the different ingredients of the quid, with or without compartments, and in rectangular, round, oval or polygonal form with different decor and made from various metals, wood or lacquer ware.

Large betel boxes to hold all the materials used for preparing betel quids and usually containing several trays. These may be made of metal or more often of bamboo and lacquer ware.

Betel bags or sacks of different material. Mainly used in some parts of Burma and in Sri Lanka.

Plates, stands and bowls for presenting betel quids to visitors or during private ceremonies.

Spittoons for collection of the red saliva produced during betel chewing. Usually wide, these are open bowls or vases made of numerous materials including metals, porcelain and lacquer ware.

---

[1] All measurements in text and figures given in centimeters.

The development of the utensils used for betel chewing in Thailand has been subject to various influences of different types. Of particular interest and significance is the fact that influences from neighbouring countries such as Burma, China, Laos and Cambodia, and to a lesser extent from Malaysia and Indonesia, have always been present. In addition, it must be remembered that the boundaries of Thailand have been subject to considerable change during the last few centuries due to numerous wars with neighbouring countries, particularly with Burma and Cambodia.

Some highlights of the history of Chiang Mai, which has been a major site for the production of utensils, may illustrate how its political fate has influenced all aspects of life, including those related to arts and handicrafts. Chiang Mai was founded by King Mang Rai in AD 1296. In 1250 the Kingdom of Ayutthaya came into being, extending its influence by invading the Kingdom of Sukothai. After several wars with Sukothai and Ayutthaya, King Phothisat of Laos claimed the throne of Chiang Mai in 1545. His son Setthathirat returned to Laos and was succeeded by a Shan prince named Maekuti who in turn surrendered to King Bayinnaung of Burma in 1556. Ayutthaya was captured by Bayinnaung in 1563. The son of Bayinnaung, Tharawadi Min, became prince of Chiang Mai after Maekuti had fled to Vientiane. After Laos declared war on Chiang Mai, Tharawadi Min was forced to appeal for assistance to Ayutthaya, with Chiang Mai thus becoming a vassal state of Ayutthaya for the first time. In 1615 Chiang Mai was recaptured by the Burmese. In 1661 Chiang Mai fell to Ayutthaya which was then driven out again by the Burmese. In 1717 the Burmese were turned out of Chiang Mai again. In 1764 Chiang Mai was taken by King Hsinbyushin of Burma. The Burmese were finally defeated in Chiang Mai in the year 1775 by King Taksin. Since the city of Chiang Mai was exhausted most of the population moved to Lampang. Chiang Mai was re-established in 1796 by Prince Kawila.

From this short survey of the lively history of Chiang Mai it becomes evident that the influences must have been extremely varied. This may be one of the reasons why the origin of some utensils found today may not be clearly identified as Northern Thai, Laotian or Burmese. It was usual for the victors in these wars to take with them craftsmen of all kinds, particularly potters, silversmiths and artists, who in turn always exported some aspects of the local artistic forms to the victorious neighbouring country. This pattern is nicely illustrated in the history of lacquer-ware in Burma, the Shan States and Northern Thailand, outlined in the next chapter.

Religion, particularly Buddhism, has had an enormous influence on art over many centuries, in Thailand as elsewhere. Buddhist iconography has been widely adapted to profane objects such as utensils used for betel quid chewing. Decorative motives and shapes such as lotus flowers and buds as well as stupas or pagodas form part of the basic designs of most objects used in the betel habit.

Fig. 35.5: Siamese king: "Supreme King of Siam in His State Robes" as published in The Land of the White Elephant: Sights and Scenes in South-East Asia, 1871–1872, *New York, Harper and Brothers, 1874. The Royal betel regalia as well as a large spittoon is seen in this print.*

Fig. 35.6: Paramindr Maha Chulalongkorn, King of Siam. The royal regalia including the betel set is seen in the background, while the spittoon is seen in the foreground. Photograph published in The Kingdom of the Yellow Robe *by Young, E., 3rd ed., London, 1907, p. 220.*

10. Characteristics of Thai Utensils

Lime containers

Lime containers have been used in many betel chewing populations. Varieties, shapes, size and materials used for lime containers are, however, enormous. Lime pots were made either as small containers for individual use or as larger pots for use in a household and for guests. As it was believed that lime could be poisoned in large containers there were many more smaller lime pots than large ones. While lime containers made of wood or bamboo such as are found in other betel quid chewing cultures are hardly found in Thailand, different metals such as gold, silver, bronze and brass were widely used for the production of those items. The materials used differed from one part of Thailand to another. Silver was widely used in most parts of Thailand for making lime containers for the wealthy, but bronze containers were used by the majority of people.

The shape of Thai lime pots shows marked influences from Buddhist iconography. The urn and chedi-like shapes are quite characteristic, as are decorative elements like the lotus bud and lotus petals. Other decorations include flowers, mythical animals and human figures, as well as simple curvilinear designs. Decoration using the repoussé or punch technique, as is widely used all over Southeast Asia, is typical (Newman, 1977). As in other Thai arts, several influences from neighbouring countries, particularly from Burma, the Shan States, Laos and Cambodia, may be traced in betel paraphernalia. This fact makes it difficult sometimes to determine the exact origin of a lime container found in Thailand. During the last 20 years, sadly, the ubiquitous plastic bag has replaced the beautiful lime containers of former times. Since the habit of betel chewing is definitely on the decline in present-day Thailand the production of the artistic lime pot of whatever material and design may soon disappear for ever.

Historical lime containers

Early specimens of lime containers or pots date back to the fourteenth to the sixteenth century of the Sukothai period. Among the numerous artefacts unearthed from the kilns of Sukothai and Si Satchanalai of central Thailand there have occasionally been lime pots of celadon or ceramic ware. These pots were usually of medium size and had the shape of urns. The lid occasionally ended in a lotus bud-like knob. The glazes varied and sometimes an underglaze decoration could be found (Spinks, 1965; van Tent, 1983, Amranand, 1986). Similar ceramic pots were later produced at Kalong and probably also at San Kamphaeng, Chiang Mai province. A typical example is illustrated in Figure 36. Small slender lime containers of bronze also dating back to the fifteenth century were found at burial sites near Tak. These containers were rather small and were shaped in typical Siamese design with a chedi- or stupa-like top to the covering lid. In Figure 37 examples of these pots, with the characteristic green / bluish patina, are shown. The shape of these lime pots could be called traditional since with some variations the basic type has continued to be made, of different materials, until recently (Shaw, 1985). A superb set of betel paraphernalia, including a lime container and areca nuts made of gold, was found at Wat Ratchaburana where it may be seen in the museum (Figs. 38, 39). Also of historical interest is the lime container of the seventeenth century shown in Figure 40.

Lime containers of silver

Silver lime containers represent the wide spectrum of shapes found in Thailand. In the northern provinces bordering the Shan States and Laos, silver containers of a high cylindrical shape were used by the Thai but also by wealthy hill tribe people (Fig. 41). A quite different shape with definite Burmese

Fig. 36 (above, left): Lime container of Kalong ceramic ware. Typical Thai urn-like shape. The everted top of this jar is surmounted with a lotus bud in relief. The cream-coloured glaze is missing on the elongated neck of the base. Similar containers were produced in Sawankhalok in Central Thailand from the fourteenth to the sixteenth century (Amranand, 1986). (Northern Thailand, late fourteenth to sixteenth century, h.: 10.0; w.: 5.8).

Fig. 37 (above, right): Lime containers of bronze from Tak hilltop burial sites. All three containers are in the shape of stupas and represent a classical Thai form. The patina of the containers varies from light greenish to blue in some parts. The lids cannot be removed from some of these containers as they are usually found filled with dried lime. On the base of the container on the left is a primitively designed animal probably representing a goat. From left to right: h.: 7.7, w.: 3.0; h.:10.4, w.: 3.3; h.: 7.7, w.: 2.8 (compare Shaw, 1985). (Central Thailand, province of Tak, late fourteenth century).

Fig. 38 (middle): Gold tray holding three gold lime boxes and the betel leaf holder from the crypt of the main prang at Wat Ratchaburana.

Fig. 39 (below): Round covered box and a bunch of areca nuts in gold; from the crypt of the main prang at Wat Ratchaburana (reprinted from Chumpengpan, 1986).

Fig. 40: Small lime container in the shape of an urn with a pagoda-like lid of thin metal foil. On a small socle with some linear engravings a voluminous body is seen covered with the elegant lid which shows decoration in the repoussé technique, showing lotus leaves and a lotus bud-like tip (h.: 9.0, w.: 4.5, 20 g) (Central Thailand, seventeenth century).

Fig. 41: Left: Lime container of silver. Lid and body connected by braided silver wire. Flower motives in repoussé technique. Lotus patterns on lid. Interior covered by dried white lime. H.: 12.6, w.: 4.4; 90 g (Northern Thailand or Laos) (compare Völger, 1984, p. 15). Right: Lime container of silver. The overlapping lid is connected to the body by loops and a braided silver wire. H.: 10.0, w.: 4.8, 142 g (compare Völger, 1984, p. 12).

Fig. 42: Left: Oval lime container of silver. Lid domed in steps with a high relief in repoussé technique showing a jumping lion or fabulous creature. Some punched minor decorations at foot of base and lid. Burmese inscriptions on base. Interior covered by dried white lime. H.: 5.9, 1.: 6.5, w.: 4.0, 132 g (compare Völger, 1984, p. 12) (Burma, Shan States). Right: Lime container of silver. Lid dome shaped with high relief in repoussé technique showing dancing warrior, probably Hanuman. H.: 5.3, l.: 6.3, w.: 4.5, 87 g (Burma; Shan States).

Fig. 43: Cylindrical lime container of silver in repoussé technique. In the centre of the lid cowering animal in high relief, surrounded by 10 flowers. In 12 rectangular frames on lid are depicted a pair of birds or a chi'i-lin which may also represent a fabulous creature. The base shows another animal in the centre of several circular incisions. H.: 5.9; w.: 5.8, 80 g (compare Völger, 1984, p. 14) (Shan States; Northern Thailand).

Fig. 44 (left): Silver container used as tobacco or betel quid container. Cylindrical shape with numerous decorations in repoussé technique. On flange of lid cross-shaped fields with birds alternating with an animal. Cross-shaped fields filled with leaf ornaments. On base in punch technique depiction of an elephant surrounded by a curvilinear floral design. H.: 10.5; w.: 11.0, 248 g (compare Lewis, 1984, p. 66 and Völger, 1984, p. 17) (Shan States; Northern Thailand).

Fig. 45 (below): Small rectangular lime container of silver. The lid is hinged on to the base. On four sides of the body rectangular fields with floral design and fruits. Silver decoration of the step-wise domed lid with four birds, one on each corner. Partly punch technique, partly application of silver and preformed elements soldered to surfaces. Base of container showing engraved flower with six petals in two circles. Some Burmese inscriptions. H.: 4.5; 1.: 5.1; w.: 3.8; 82 g (Shan States; Burma or Northern Thailand).

influence is shown in Figure 42. The lids are often decorated with animals and human figures. Larger containers also found in the provinces bordering the Shan States often reveal a very delicate decoration (Figs. 43, 44). An elegant rectangular type of lime or areca nut container with Burmese influence is shown in Figure 45. Different and often octagonal in shape are silver lime boxes which were made by Chinese craftsmen who probably lived in Thailand. The containers are decorated by stylised floral designs that are often repeated on the different facets of the containers. Figure 46 is representative of typical examples of these containers which were mostly used in Northern and Central Thailand.

Some containers in the shape of vegetables or pumpkins as shown in Figure 47 have their origin in Cambodia, but were also used in neighbouring parts of Thailand. These containers were rather small, although larger examples do exist. An example of such a container is shown in Figure 48. Figure 49 shows a peculiar shape of container also made of silver. Betel paraphernalia have been collectors' items for a long time and Figure 50 shows lime pots and other betel objects which were in the possession of Reginald le May who travelled to Northern Thailand in the early years of the twentieth century. The right and left lime containers are examples of pots peculiar to Northern Thailand.

In the northern province of Chiang Mai and bordering areas the use of an alloy called *pan ca*, which is made of several materials including silver, gold, brass and copper, resulted in the production of black lime pots which were often decorated with silver using the repoussé technique. Two different examples of lime pots of this alloy are shown in Figures 51 and 52.

Lime containers of bronze or brass

Containers made of bronze and more rarely of brass are still quite common in Thailand. These are often quite large and have been in use until very recently (Figs. 53–55). Many of these lime containers have been made in the shape of urns. While some of these elegant containers do not show elements of decoration (Figs. 56, 57, 59) others reveal simple decorative patterns (Fig. 58). Most of these containers have been made by the lost-wax procedure, while some have been produced from thin sheeting and show lines of soldering (Fig. 60). Rather simple lime containers of metal are occasionally found among the hill tribes of Northern Thailand (Fig. 61). An example of a lime container common in Cambodia and neighbouring Thailand is depicted in Figure 62.

Lime containers of porcelain

Lime containers of porcelain were also used in Thailand. These were often imported from China, sometimes being examples of Ming or later periods (Fig. 63).

Spatulas

Spatulas used to spread lime onto the betel leaves have probably not been as much in use among Thai as in other betel quid chewing cultures. Usually, spatulas are of rather small size and often made of bronze. Handles may be quite simple, but may be shaped in the form of birds or human beings or be of geometrical design. Figure 64 shows some examples of spatulas found in the province of Chiang Mai, some of which may, however, be of Burmese origin. Large spatulas as used in Malaysia are not encountered in Thailand. In Sri Lanka, where betel chewing is still prevalent, spatulas are usually chained to the chunam (lime) container.

Areca nut cutters

The cutters of Thailand, Malaysia and Indonesia form a discrete group with basic differences from those of India, Sri Lanka, China and Burma. Brownrigg in his recent (1991) publication has elaborated on these differences:

> In the latter countries, such as India, Sri Lanka, China, a variety of metals are used, and, more importantly, the handles are part of the overall structure. By con-

Fig. 46: Tall octagonal silver lime container. Body and lid with rectangular fields showing stylised leaves in punch and repoussé techniques. Bottom of container with Chinese mark. Inner surfaces covered with white dried lime. H.: 6.5; w.: 2.9; 38 g (Southern China or Northern Thailand). Right: Flat octagonal lime container of silver. In small rectangular frames the body shows plants, flowers and birds in repoussé technique. The lid shows two flowers with a bird in repoussé technique. Bottom of base shows a Chinese mark. H.: 3.2; l.: 4.7; 31 g (Southern China or Northern Thailand).

Fig. 47: Three small silver lime containers, spherical in shape, with flat poles probably representing a fruit or vegetable such as mangosteen or pumpkin. Base and lid are decorated by punch technique, in some instances representing lotus petals (see lid on lower container). The lids are decorated by layers of leaves with a short stem, also decorated by punch technique (from left to right to front: h.: 3.0, d.: 4.1, 18 g; h.: 2.8, d.: 4.7, 28 g; h.: 2.6, d.: 3.7, 14 g (compare Thierry, 1969, p. 247) (Cambodia; Central and Southeast Thailand).

Fig. 48: Container made of silver in the form of a pumpkin. The lid takes up the decoration of the body; the surface is decorated with small engravings, giving the appearance of the surface of a fruit. On the top three filigree leaves are held together with a small cylindrical stem (h.:7.8, l.: 12.5, 152 g) (Cambodia).

Fig. 49: Betel nut container of silver, semi-cylindrical in shape, with lid fixed by a hinge. Decoration in repoussé technique with rectangular vignettes showing birds and foliage, which are also seen on the lid (Shan States; Northern Thailand; h.: 3.5, l.: 8.7, w.: 5.2, 82.3 g).

Fig. 50: Group of utensils for chewing betel nut, including six lime pots, nut crackers, holder for the betel leaf, pestle and mortar for pounding the nut. Reprinted from Le May, 1926, pp. 196–197.

Fig. 51: Lime container in the shape of a stupa on a conical base partly decorated in repoussé technique. Neck of body elongated and covered by lid. On top, motive in the shape of a cylindrical button. H.: 19.5, w.: 7.2 (Thierry, 1969, p. 197) (Northern Thailand).

Fig. 52: Small lime container of oval shape made of pan ca, a typical alloy of different metals including silver, gold, brass and copper and characterised by its black colour. Body and lid decorated by small silver ledges. On top of lid a silver floral motive in repoussé technique. H.: 4.7, w.: 5.4 (compare Thierry, 1969, p. 196) (Northern Thailand).

Fig. 53: Large lime container of bronze. Different alloys were used for the cover and the body. Cylindrical shape with truncated cone at the base. Bands of ornaments at the base and on the lid covering the elongated neck. Small loop on the top of the lid as well as on the base of the container. Both loops were usually connected by a chain to prevent loss of the lid. Interior surface covered by pink lime. H.: 20.4; w.: 6.5 (Northeast Thailand, early twentieth century) (compare Thierry, 1969, p. 212).

Fig. 54: Left: Cylindrical lime container of bronze. Body and lid decorated by bands of V-shaped incisions as well as stylised circular motives. Similar decoration of the flat conical top of the lid. This type of lime container usually has a small hole in the centre of the base. H.: 15.8, w.: 4.8 (Northeast Thailand). Right: This type of lime container of bronze was used until recently. Shaped like an urn with stupa-like top of lid. Circular engravings at the base and on lid. H.: 19.2, w.: 7.0 (Northern and Central Thailand, twentieth century).

Fig. 55: Lime pot of yellow brass with a conical socle and a spherical body covered with a lid in steps ending in a lotus bud. The shape is reminiscent of a funeral urn. H.: 10.0, w.: 7.0 (compare Thierry, 1969, p. 236) (Thailand, twentieth century).

Fig. 56 (opposite, top left): Elegant lime container of bronze in the shape of a stupa or urn. On a small socle a short voluminous base is joined by a long slender lid ending in a lotus bud. Dark greenish patina. H.: 17.8, w.: 6.2 (compare Thierry, 1969, p. 237) (Northern or Central Thailand, twentieth century).

Fig. 57 (opposite, top right): Two lime pots of bronze, both without surface decoration. Left: Elegant lime pot on a small socle with a rather short body and a long slender cover. The cover or lid ends in four steps with a lotus bud-like knob on top. Interior shows traces of white and pink lime (h.: 10.5, w.: 3.5; cf. Thierry, 1969, p. 237). (Northern Thailand, Laos, probably also Cambodia). Right: Similar container with a more conical end to the top in five steps. The surface of this container is shiny with a dark brown-black patina (h.: 9.2, w.: 3.4) (Northern Thailand; Laos).

Fig. 58 (opposite, lower right): Lime pot of bronze in the shape of a cylindrical urn. Decoration of incised circles and semicircles on the base and cover. The latter is decorated with incised lotus petals in steps. On top a small loop serves for a chain or cord which can be connected to the body. Pink lime in the inner part (h.: 11.5, w.: 3.2; compare Thierry, 1969, p. 212) (Northern Thailand; Laos).

Fig. 59 (opposite, lower middle): Lime pot of bronze in the shape of an urn with smooth undecorated surface. From a flat socle a rather voluminous body and corresponding lid make up this container. The top of the lid consists of three steps ending in a stylised lotus bud (h.: 11.0, w.: 5.8) (Central Thailand, nineteenth century).

Fig. 60 (opposite, lower right): Lime container of bronze sheet. Lower part of the body as well as lid show a fine line of soldering from the bottom to the tip of the container. Upper part of the lid in steps decorated with a lotus motif. Traces of lime inside (Northern or Central Thailand, nineteenth century).

trast in Thailand, Malaysia and Indonesia all cutters are made of iron, with other metals appearing solely as decoration. The iron handles are plain and are almost always sheathed in tubes of gold, silver or white metal. These sheaths are often finely worked but they are of different workmanship from the cutters themselves, and the cutter therefore becomes the sum of two parts rather than an integrated whole. This is exacerbated by the fact that the sheaths often get damaged or lost and are replaced with others which are not original.

Areca nut cutters from Thailand mostly originate from the southern part of the country which had long political and cultural links with West Malaysia. Comparable to the overlap of designs in other parts of Thailand (in the north with Burma and in the east with Cambodia), there is a shared style for the areca nut cutter, essentially Thai in origin. Brownrigg nicely describes this:

> Cutters of the Thai/Malaysian type are all of roughly the same form, which is slender, boat-shaped and generally smaller and less robust than cutters from the Indian subcontinent. At the hinge end is the head of a mythical monster, whose jaw and crest move when the cutter is used. In Malaysian examples this head is sometimes stylised into an abstract or semi-abstract form in deference to the Islamic dislike of figurative representation. The animal's tail is shown as a spike jutting forwards from the blade arm near the handle. In Thai/Malaysian cutters this tail is either vestigial or is highly stylised so as to resemble a typical Thai flame motif.
>
> The handles are sheathed in gold, silver or white metal, sometimes with niello decoration. Niello work, often combined with silver gilt, was a speciality of the town of Nakorn Si Thammarat in South Thailand, from where the technique spread to the Malaysian state of Kedah. The sheaths end in finials which vary from characteristically Thai lotus buds to the round and parasol shapes found in Malaysia and in Indonesia.

The simplest and most common form of areca nut cutter operates like a small guillotine with a vertical movement suitable for paring the hard fruit. As stated before, cutters were usually made of iron and decorated with silver or other metals. A typical design is shown in Figure 65, with the representation of a dragon head so characteristic of Thailand. Other areca nut cutters of iron are shown in Figures 66–68 which show some decoration. Areca nut cutters from Burma come in two rather distinct styles (Brownrigg, 1991). While the more common type comes from upper Burma the second style is likely to have originated in the coastal area of Arakan. The cutters of the first style are rather simple and are characterised by flat handles rounded at the tip. The blade is straight. The inner edge of the blade arm forms an acute angle with the blade and has a nose-like projection about one-third of the way down. This type of cutter is decorated with silver, brass or copper wire in scrolling meanders or bird designs. The second type is characterised by a very pronounced saddle-back form of the blade arm with the handle bending back from a high shoulder. The nose-like projection becomes a hook, echoing the curve of the blade. Three examples of Burmese areca nut cutters which were exported to India but also in use in Northern Thailand are shown in Figures 69–71.

In his monograph on betel cutters Brownrigg states that knives for cutting areca nuts in Thailand do not seem to figure in the betel sets of the royal collection. During many years of surveying betel paraphernalia in Northern and Central Thailand the present authors also found the occurrence of knives as part of betel sets to be very uncommon. When used for cutting the areca nut, these knives have a particular shape, adapted to the use of cutting the areca nut into small pieces (Figs. 72, 73).

Of interest are some speculations about the areca nut cutter through the ages. Morarjee (1974) notes that although evidence establishes that betel nut chewing has been known in India at least since the fifth century AD, no evidence has so far been

Fig. 61: Small simple lime container, probably of bronze, not cast but made of sheeting about 1.5 mm thick. Brownish patina on surface. Heavy encrustations with white lime in the interior (Karen hill tribe, Northern Thailand; h.: 5.3, d.: 3.4).

Fig. 63: Porcelain vase used as lime container. Blue underglaze floral motives with some cracking of the surface. White lime in the interior (h.: 4.6, w.: 7.2) (blue and white Chinese porcelain, probably of Ming period as used in Thailand).

Fig. 62: Lime container of bell metal. The perforated base contains a small mobile metal ball. This bell type resembles Buddha amulets which always contain a small metal grain. The lid ends in a small lotus bud. H.: 12.7, w.: 3.8 (compare Thierry, 1969, p. 237) (Southeast Thailand bordering on Cambodia; and Cambodia).

Fig. 64: *Different lime spatulas of bronze. From left to right: Simple spatula with slender ovoid handle ending in four circular rings and knob. Heavily encrusted lime spatula with mythical bird as handle (see also specimen on the far right). Lime spatula with a small female figure as a handle. H.: (from left to right) 11.5, 11.2, 11.4, 8.2 (Burma or Northern Thailand).*

Fig. 65: *Top: Areca nut cutter of iron in a traditional Thai form representing the head of a dragon. The blade and body are decorated by curvilinear engravings. The eye of the dragon serves as the hinge with the mouth of the dragon opening and closing. The handles of this type of areca nut cutter are often decorated with silver applications. They may have been lost from this piece (compare Thierry, 1969, pp. 181 and 198). L.: 12.5, h.: 5.0 (Northern or Central Thailand). Bottom: Areca nut cutter of iron with large blade and slightly curved back. The blade fits in between two curved arches of the opposite branch. The axis seems to form the eye of a stylised animal. Some curvilinear engravings (compare Thierry, 1969, p. 218). L.: 11.5, h.: 4.5 (Northern Thailand).*

Fig. 66: *Although quite crude the hinge of this cutter as well as the corresponding part of one branch gives the impression of a bird's head. L.: 17.0, h.: 5.5 (Northern or Central Thailand).*

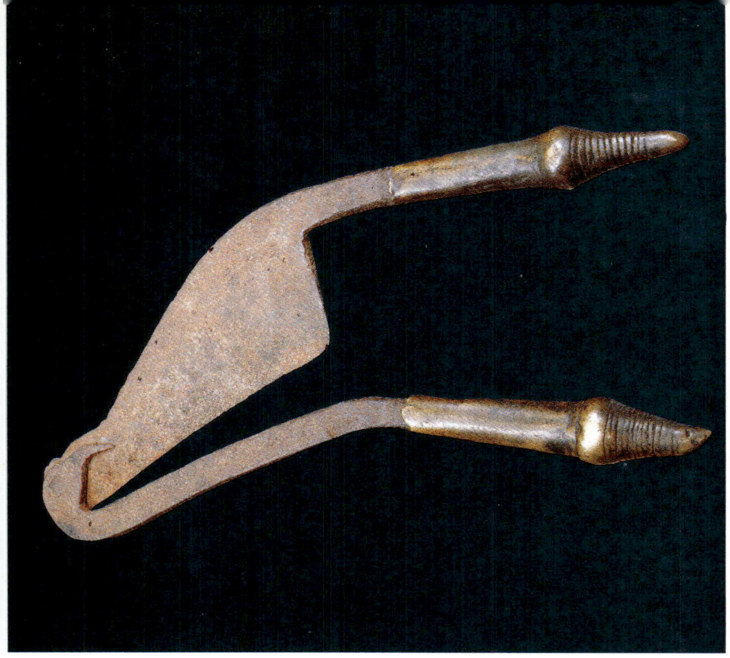

Fig. 67: Nut cutter of iron, handles decorated with brass. This cutter is characterised by a rather large blade, the dorsum of which is slightly bent. The hinge, as in many other examples is reminiscent of the eye of a bird's head. Some remnants of linear decoration incised in the blade and the counterblade are still present. The handles end in a conical shape with some simple linear decoration (l.: 19.0, h.: 5.4) (Central or Northern Thailand).

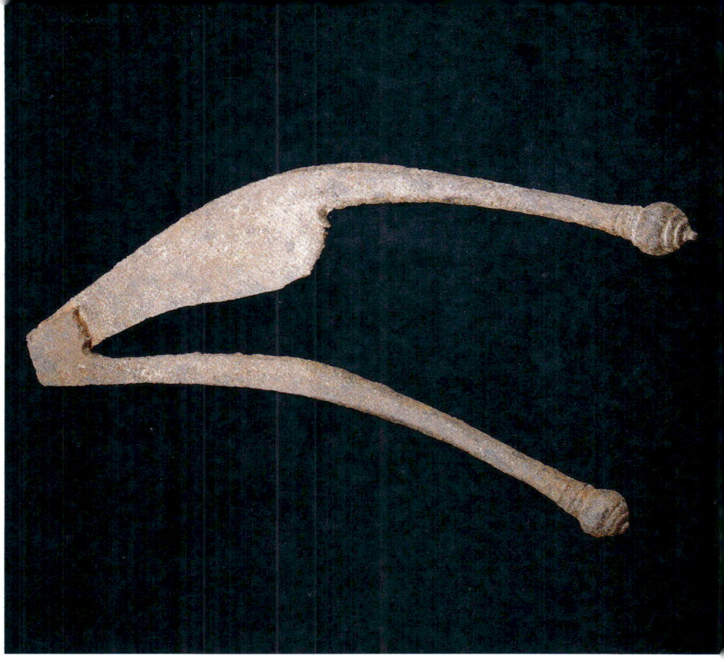

Fig. 68: Betel nut cutter of iron covered by rust. Traces of incision on upper and lower arm. Handles end in round knobs in the shape of lotus buds (l.: 22.5) (probable excavation piece, Sukothai period?, Central Thailand).

Fig. 69: Areca nut cutter in the form of a cock. Elegant in shape, this cutter reveals remnants of gold and silver applications. The hinge of the cutter represents the eye of the cock. Although the cock as a mythical bird is also found in Northern Thailand it is more prevalent in Burma. L.: 13.3, h.: 4.5 (Burma or Northern Thailand).

Fig. 70: Betel nut cutter of iron with brass inlay and mounts. This rather elegant betel nut cutter in principle follows the so-called "saddle-back" style of Burmese betel nut cutters. However it is not as curved, revealing a straighter shape. A stylised bird is attached by a pin to the blade arm (Burma, l.: 14.5; compare Brownrigg, 1991, p. 92).

Fig. 71: Betel nut cutter of bell metal, including the blade. The blade arm is decorated with two birds on each side in a dot-stamped fashion. Foliar decoration on the lower blade. Burmese inscription on the inner aspect of the upper blade (Burma; compare Brownrigg, 1991, p. 94).

Fig. 72: Areca nut knife of iron, wood and silver. The blade and handle form an angle of about 20 degrees to facilitate the cutting of areca nuts. The handle of black-brownish wood is decorated with silver in repoussé technique (compare Thierry, 1969, p. 218). L.: 24.6 (Central Thailand).

Fig. 73: Two areca nut knives as used in Thailand. The larger (above) is fitted with an iron blade and a handle made of brass. The slightly bent form of the knife is typical. The decoration of the handle is primitive, showing circles in a row (l.: 25.7). Both handle and blade of the lower knife are brass. The handle is decorated with an open-frame spiral decoration. The blade is fitted into a handle with a small piece of wood (l.: 18.6) (both objects Central or Northern Thailand).

Fig. 74: Pounder, ta ban mak, and pestle made of bronze. The tubular or conical shaped pounder shows some simple incised decorations. The pestle is made of iron with a round flat handle made of bronze. Common and simple type for crushing areca nuts in North and Northeast Thailand. Pounder h.: 12.2; pestle h.: 13.0 (compare Thierry, 1969, p. 204).

Fig. 75: Pounder of bronze with pestle of wood and iron. Surface decoration with incised lines and bands as well as floral motives representing lotus flowers. The wooden handle of the pestle shows the head of an animal or fish. The pestle itself is in the form of a screwdriver. Pounder h.: 16.8; pestle h.: 19.8 (Northern Thailand (Chiang Mai)).

Fig. 76: Conical pounder of bronze with pestle of iron and bone. Black-greenish patina with circumlinear incisions as decorations. The handle of the pestle is in the shape of a bird. Remnants of lime within the pounder and on the pestle. Pounder h.: 12.6; pestle h.: 17.3 (Northern Thailand).

Fig. 77: Pounder and pestle of bronze. Curvilinear engravings decorate the pounder. Remnants of lime visible on interior surface. Knob-like pestle handle with similar decoration. The end of the pestle bi-dented. This pounder has probably been used for a long time and may date back to the middle of the nineteenth century. Pounder h.: 9.5; pestle h.: 13.3 (Central Thailand).

Fig. 78: Two mortars and one small spatula (spoon). From left to right: Small spoon of brass with incrustations of lime (l.: 7.9); Mortar of brass cast in lost-wax technique with linear and curvilinear decoration on surface (h.: 7.4, w. at opening: 3.2); Another mortar of bronze similar in shape and design. Both mortars show traces of lime in the interior (h.: 7.5, w. at opening: 3.6) (Central or Northern Thailand, probably eighteenth century).

found to indicate that nut cutters were used then. Based on some historical Kannada inscriptions and some early references to the words *adkotu* and *adketii* occurring in the Basvapurana of Himakavi composed in AD 1369, Gode postulated that nut cutters had definitely been in existence since the fourteenth century. In the Eilenberg collection an areca nut cutter of iron with copper sheathing and silver inlay dating back to AD 1400 was described, having been excavated in Sukothai, Central Thailand (Brownrigg, 1991).

Areca nut pounders

Pounders are used either to crush the areca nut or to mix the entire quid. Areca nut pounders are usually of cylindrical shape and made of metal such as bronze or brass. Pestles with a flattened knob-like handle are made of iron, often with a screwdriver-like or indented end to improve the efficiency of this utensil. Characteristically, the mortars are closed by a piece of wood. Decoration is usually simple with incised lines or curvilinear designs in floral pattern (Figs. 74–76). Occasionally, more intricate patterns are found (Figs. 77, 78). Pounders are produced by the lost-wax casting process. While mortars made from bronze have been used in most parts of Thailand, in the south the technique of Niello was used to decorate mortars in particular (Figs. 79, 80). Niello or *tompat* in Thai is a specific type of decoration of silver or bronze with designs on a black background. The design is first hammered into the surface of the object and cleaned with a graving tool. The black substance, which is a compound of several metals with a lower melting point than for example silver, is placed in the depressions of this pattern in the form of a powder. The object is then subjected to heat until the black filling melts. The surface is filed down, scraped and polished, with the design appearing in a delicate form of silver or bronze on a black background. Nakhon Si Thammarat, in Southern Thailand, has been a centre for this technique. The handles of pestles have been designed of different materials such as horn, wood, bone or metal and often the shapes of fish or cocks (Fig. 81) have been used.

Betel leaf holders

Betel leaf holders as used in Thailand were usually of bronze, silver or made from lacquer-ware. Leaf holders were often part of a set of different containers and had the shape of rectangular cornucopias (Fig. 82) or flattened horns of plenty (Fig. 83). When made of silver the repoussé and punch technique was used for decoration, often in combination with open work or perforated technique (Fig. 84). Leaf holders made from silver were used in the central and northern part of Thailand. In the northern provinces leaf holders were also made from lacquer-ware (Fig. 85). These were usually decorated in a typical northern style, using black and red lacquer alone. Lacquer-ware in different colours as used in Burma was not favoured in the northern provinces.

Lacquer-ware boxes

Lacquer-ware originated in China, reaching its full significance in terms of technique and artistic design during the Chou period (eleventh century BC to third century AD). While lacquer-ware had a tradition in China of almost 2,500 years, its history in Northern Thailand and Burma is less clear. However, it is likely that lacquer-ware craftsmanship was introduced to Southeast Asia with the emigration of the Thai, since early centres for the art of lacquer-ware existed in present-day Laos and Northern Thailand. From here the technique of lacquer-ware was most probably introduced to Burma. It has been suggested that the craft of lacquer-ware was introduced from Northern Siam to central Burma during the eleventh century by the Mon. This was interpreted as a consequence of the Burmese conquest of the Mon city of Thaton and the abduction of Mon craftsmen to the city of Pagan. However, it has been stated that the typical lacquer-ware of the Mon was made without ornaments, thus being

Fig. 79: Pounder and pestle of Niello ware. Small tubular pounder with decorations of floral and linear pattern. Pestle with knob-like handle with corresponding decoration. Pounder h.: 7.8, pestle h.: 9.5 (Southern Thailand).

Fig. 80 (opposite, top left): Large pounder and pestle of Niello ware. Floral design on body of pounder. The long iron pestle has a highly polished handle of buffalo horn. Pounder h.: 20.5, pestle h.: 26.0 (Southern Thailand).

Fig. 81 (opposite, top right): Three mortars and pounders as found in one of Chiang Mai's antique shops (Maneesinn Antiques). While the left piece is representative of the common mortars and pestles the other two show some special features. The pestle in the middle was fitted with a bird's figure carved of ivory, whereas the mortar to the right was made of bone and the pestle was of black wood (Chiang Mai, Thailand).

Fig. 82 (opposite, below): Betel leaf holder of silver in the form of a horn of plenty, right-angled in cross-section; the opening trapezoid. On all four surfaces decorations in repoussé technique with floral motives and animal representing a mythical lion. H.: 9.2, o. (=opening): 5.2 x 3.8, 44 g (compare Thierry, 1969, p. 203) (Laos; Northern Thailand).

Fig. 83: Betel leaf holder of silver in a flattened horn-like shape with a small, perforated hexagonal base. Decoration in repoussé technique showing Chinese man in landscape with tree. In other fields floral and foliage design. On base two Chinese marks. H.: 11.8, o.: 7.5, 68 g (compare Verwilghen, 1985, pp. 98-105, and Thierry, 1969, p. 228) (Southern China to Thailand).

Fig. 84 (opposite): Close-up of decorations of silver betel leaf holders of Chinese or Northern Thai origin. Top left, perforated or open work decoration with foliage, birds and a fish. Below left, open-work decoration with punch technique showing landscape with tree and foliage as well as floral motives. Top right, repoussé technique with additional punch technique, flowers and foliage interrupted by simple punch-marked bands. Below right, repoussé technique with curl-like motive which is known from Buddhist iconography.

Fig. 85: Betel leaf holder of horn-like shape of lacquer-ware. Exterior in black and red lacquer with a floral design incised into the black surface. Interior in red lacquer. H.: 9.7, o.: 7.5 (Northern Thailand).

Fig. 86: Flat betel lacquer box with one inset in red and black lacquer. The ornaments on this lacquer box are comparatively simple, showing a curvilinear pattern in the form of a trefoil arched frieze (Junnan semi-circle design). The centre shows a small medallion with a design of leaves. The bottom of the box shows some Burmese inscriptions in the centre. H.: 9.0, d.: 18.1 (lacquer box with design type I, Prunner, 1966; cellular design) (Burma).

Fig. 87: Small betel container of red and black lacquer with two insets. The decoration on the red background is simple with the typical trefoil arched frieze motif (h.: 9.0, d.: 12.6) (Burma; Shan States).

quite different from the lacquer-ware of Northern Thailand and Burma. In addition, it has been suggested that lacquer-ware was introduced to Burma during the reign of King Bayinnaung in the sixteenth century. Deportation of craftsmen from the state of Chiang Mai was the means whereby this technique was introduced to Burma. While present-day knowledge does not permit a definitive answer to the question of when and how the technique of lacquer-ware was introduced into Burma or Northern Siam, it is obvious that Chiang Mai is still a centre for lacquer-ware production today. There have been influences in both directions—from Burma and Thailand—on the art and design of lacquer-ware. Thus, today it is difficult to determine the origin of some of the lacquer boxes found in museums and collections.

The basic material, the lacquer, is the sap of a tree, Melanhorrea usitata. Lacquer boxes to hold betel quid ingredients are usually made of woven or plaited bamboo or of plaited horse hair, and the shape of the box may take various forms. The base object, with its lids and trays is sealed with layers of lacquer to fill the interstices. After drying, the object is polished to obtain a smooth and shiny surface. Several more layers, sometimes in different colours, are applied to the object. Finally, designs are engraved or etched into the surface. The designs are extremely various. For Burmese lacquer-ware, however, four larger categories of decoration have been proposed. Type I is reminiscent of the trefoil arched frieze design; type II is similar to type I in that it includes the trefoil arched frieze, but the background decoration is much more intricate and richly ornamented (Figs. 86, 87). Type III lacks the trefoil arched frieze but has instead a medallion frieze. Type IV is characterised by the depiction of figures of animals or human beings (Figs. 88, 89) (Prunner, 1966; Fraser-Lu, 1985). Betel boxes that are probably of Burmese origin are often characterised by several different colours such as red, black, yellow and green (Figs. 90–93). The different parts of a lacquer betel box including lid, base and insets are shown in Figure 94. The typical betel leaf design is illustrated in Figure 95.

Lacquer boxes and containers for betel quid ingredients in Northern Thailand are most often decorated by layers of black and red lacquer. A typical example is shown in Figure 96 which is decorated with a floral pattern (called the Chiang Mai style in Burma) plus the animals of the zodiac. In rural communities simple black lacquer boxes were used for offering betel quid to guests (Fig. 97). The double layer technique of black and red lacquer with the floral motives typical of the northern part of Thailand is also applied to the small containers which are used in a betel set (Figs. 98, 99). Spittoons, though rarely made of lacquer-ware, may also reveal the characteristic floral decoration in a black and red lacquer technique (Fig. 100). While betel boxes and sets made of lacquer have been produced in large quantities, containers for *miang*[1] (which is a fermented tea and chewed in a similar fashion to a betel quid) are not as frequently found.

Figure 101 shows a small dome-shaped lacquer box of Burmese origin which was most probably used for fermented tea.

Lacquer-ware is still produced in Burma and Northern Thailand. With the gradual disappearance of the betel chewing habit the art and technique of producing betel boxes of lacquer-ware may also slowly vanish.

Betel sets and stands

Betel sets differ considerably in material and artistic value according to the social status of the owner and his or her location within Thailand. While royal regalia were, and still are, made of gold (Brus, 1985), princely families also had in their possession betel sets of gold and silver (Fig. 102). Often plates or stands were of precious metals and decorated with rubies or other precious or semi-precious stones (Fig. 103). Silver sets were quite common, usually deco-

[1] *Miang* is described in Chapter 11.

Fig. 88: Betel box in red, green and black lacquer with two inset trays. The top of the lid shows four running elephants and five human figures. The central figure seems to dance. The side of the lid shows figures of elephants, palms and men, some with bow and arrow. Bottom of trays and box decorated with circular incisions and floral motive in the centre. H.: 18.5, d.: 21.5 (type IV, Burmese betel box; Prunner, 1966) (Burma; Shan States).

Fig. 89: Lacquer betel box in black, red and yellow lacquer with one inset tray. Motives of black elephants and men on top of lid with clear red margins over a yellowish net-like ornament. The side of the lid shows a similar decoration including birds and monkeys. Bottom of box carries circular incisions with a bird in the centre. H.: 19.0, d.: 21.2 (type IV of Burmese lacquer boxes; Prunner, 1966) (Burma; Shan States).

Fig. 90: Lacquer box in black, red and yellow lacquer. The box consists of a basal, central and lid part. In addition, two inset trays of black and red lacquer. The lid with short sides reveals variation of a human figure on a net-like red background with yellow curly motives. The side of the central part reveals floral motives in black, red and yellow. Untreated yellowish strips of bamboo on all three parts of the body. Black and brown circular decoration on the bottom of the base with central medallion with rosette. H.: 18.8, d.: 21.4 (Burmese lacquer box with decoration type IV; Prunner, 1966) (Burma; Shan States).

Fig. 91: Betel lacquer box in black, red and yellow lacquer with two inset trays. The side of the body is decorated with a scene depicting warriors elegantly dancing. A similar decoration is found on the cover. The decorations were made using the characteristic incision technique (h.: 20.5, d.: 20.5) (Burma; Shan States).

Fig. 92: Lacquer betel box in red and black lacquer in three parts with two inset trays. Top of lid shows three pagodas in incision technique. The side of the central part reveals floral patterns in rosettes. Strips of unlacquered bamboo are indented on all three parts of the body. Bottom of box is partly gilded with a floral design and a small central rosette. H.: 16.5, d.: 16.2 (Burma; Shan States).

Fig. 93: Lacquer betel box with two insets of black, red, yellow and green lacquer. The yellow and red decoration is of curvilinear type with some stylised animals and human figures. These are found on the side of the lid as well as on top of the box (h.: 13.0, d.: 14.5) (Burma; Shan States).

Fig. 94: Betel lacquer box showing the insets in which the betel quid ingredients were kept (Burma or Northern Thailand, nineteenth century).

Fig. 95: Detail of a lacquer box in betel leaf pattern. The betel leaves are in black and the elegant tip of the leaf is clearly shown (Burma or Northern Thailand, nineteenth century).

Fig. 96: Betel lacquer box in black and red lacquer with one inset tray. The side of the body is decorated with the twelve animals of the zodiac. Floral design and foliage in the so-called Chiang Mai style (compare Fraser-Lu, 1985, pp. 47, 50). Characteristic incision technique with the black figures standing on the red underground. H.: 12.0, d.: 25.5 (Northern Thailand).

Fig. 97: Betel lacquer box in three parts with two inset trays. Note incised decoration of solely black lacquer. Some relief moulding on upper lower part of box. H.: 26.0, d.: 31.0 (Northern Thailand).

Fig. 98: Lid of small container for betel quid components as part of a betel set. Characteristic black and red lacquer with floral design as applied on Northern Thai lacquer ware. H.: 3.2, d.: 6.1 (Northern Thailand).

Fig. 99: Top of lid of small lacquer box belonging to a betel set in black and red lacquer. Several leaves are in the shape of betel leaves. The sides of the box are decorated with similar motives. H.: 2.8, d.: 5.1 (Northern Thailand).

Fig. 100: Spittoon of black and red lacquer. The interior is covered by red lacquer. The outer surface decorated by the incision technique revealing floral pattern with foliage sometimes reminiscent of the shape of betel leaves. H.: 9.3, d. of opening: 15.0 (Northern Thailand).

Fig. 101: Lacquer box most probably used for fermented tea leaves (miang; Burmese le'hpe'). A largely convex body with inset and lid. Bottom shows a central circle of black lacquer with Burmese character. H.: 7.5, d.: 10.0 (Burma; Shan States).

Fig. 102: Betel tray with three containers for betel ingredients; silver gilded. Tray decorated in repoussé technique with floral design and foliage. Six feet representing butterflies. Three betel containers in the form of vegetable or pumpkin with floral design in repoussé technique. Each container top is decorated with two or three layers of leaves and a short stem representing a stem of a fruit. On the bottom of each container is a small Chinese mark. Tray h.: 4.0, d.: 19.9, 134 g. Containers (from right to left) h.: 3.7, d.: 5.5, 51 g, h.: 4.0, d.: 6.0, 53 g and h.: 4.3, d.: 6.5, 70 g (Chinese, probably made and used in Central Thailand).

Fig. 103: Gilded stand for offering betel quids to guests. Indented rim of plate, inlaid with rubies. The stand in open-work decoration with incised floral design. H.: 16.0, d. of plate: 21.5, d. of stand: 10.8, 750 g (Central Thailand).

Fig. 104: Complete silver betel set with bowl, three containers of different sizes, a leaf holder and a small cup to mix different betel ingredients. An areca nut cutter of iron with handles covered in silver and ending in a lotus-like knob makes the set complete. The cutter is in the typical shape of a dragon. All parts of the set are decorated by repoussé technique with the curl-like protuberances characteristic of Buddhist iconography (Northern and Central Thailand).

Fig. 105: Betel set of silver on wooden container for paraphernalia. The leaf container of pure silver is of a characteristic shape used in Laos. Floral design in punch technique (inhomogenous set of partly Laotian, partly Chinese origin).

Fig. 106: Betel set with tray and three larger containers, a small flat bowl and a simple leaf container, all made of bronze. In the centre is an urn-shaped lime container which does not belong to the set. The three larger containers are shaped as stupas of different heights. The leaf container is of characteristic form as found in Thailand. This type of betel set has been used until recently (Northern and Central Thailand).

Fig. 107: Complete betel set of black and red lacquer with a large betel box, four smaller containers in the shape of a pumpkin with a small conical handle, a betel leaf container and a cup-like device. All items are decorated by floral patterns and foliage in the incision technique characteristic of Northern Thai lacquer ware (Northern Thailand).

Fig. 108: Betel set parts of which are shown in Figures 85 and 96. The animals of the zodiac are shown on the outer surface of the box together with a simple floral design. The smaller containers are characteristic of Northern Thai lacquer ware (Northern Thailand).

Fig. 109: Betel set of wood in simple rectangular form with five compartments. Simple wooden lids to each of these compartments (Thailand).

Fig. 110: Betel set of plaited rattan material. Large box with lid and four smaller containers of the same material. Remnants of red lacquer on box and small containers (Northern Thailand).

Fig. 111: Octagonal betel stand of plaited bamboo covered with red and black lacquer. This comparatively small betel box of unusual shape contains two insets for betel quid ingredients. The eight walls of the container have been decorated with red lacquer in linear and floral design (Northern Thailand).

Fig. 112: Betel container and stand of wood, square in shape with a lower and upper pyramidal part. The upper part with a wooden bottom reveals four compartments for the different betel ingredients. Rims are covered with narrow list of bone. Inlay work with bone on all four sides. The wood has been treated with a thin layer of lacquer. H.: 15.5, l.: 23.5, w.: 23.0 (compare Locke, 1976, pp. 25–29) (Northeast Thailand).

Fig. 113: Betel stand typical of the Isan area. Four compartments allow for the separation of the different betel ingredients. The surface of this wooden stand is covered with black and red lacquer and some simple carvings. Pieces of bone have been used to cover the rims of the compartments (Northeast Thailand).

Fig. 114: Another example of the betel stands found in Northeast Thailand. This example shows a black lacquer background covered with some floral and linear red lacquer (Northeast Thailand).

Fig. 115: Postcard issued by Thai Airways International (1990), showing a silver betel set with gilded areca nut cutter. The betel set is presented as reflecting a bygone age.

Fig. 116: Plaited and lacquered betel container produced by the Karen hill tribe. Made of woven bamboo it is fitted inside with two shallow trays. The interior is roughly lacquered with black lacquer. The sides of the box are decorated with partly indented strips of yellow bamboo. H.: 10.0, d.: 9.2 (compare Lewis, 1984, p. 272) (Karen hill tribes of Burma and Northern Thailand).

Fig. 117: Oval black woven box or container used for betel quid ingredients by Lahu hill tribes. The roughly plaited bamboo material is covered with a thin layer of black lacquer. H.: 6.0, l.: 12.5, w.: 7.4 (Lewis, 1984, p. 276) (Northern Thailand).

Fig. 118: Betel or tobacco container made of bamboo and wood used by the Akha hill tribe. The sides of the base and the lid are made of bamboo and are fixed by bamboo threads. Some nails have been used to fix a bamboo rim at the base and the lid (Lewis, 1984, p. 280) (Akha hill tribe, Northern Thailand).

rated in the repoussé and punch technique, and consisting of several small containers for lime, tobacco and areca nut, a small cup for mixing the ingredients, a betel leaf container and an areca nut cutter (Fig. 104). A simpler set is shown in Figure 105 which consists of several small boxes of silver with a betel leaf container on a tray made of wood. During the last few decades trays made of bronze, as shown in Figure 106, were common in households in Central and Northern Thailand. Containers showed the typical form of stupas or pagodas as found in temples in Thailand. Betel sets of wood, lacquer or of woven bamboo or rattan were found in rural households of Northern and Central Thailand. Lacquer-ware was decorated in the Chiang Mai style and the lacquer colours were restricted to red and black (Figs. 107–108). Examples of betel set boxes of wood and woven rattan are shown in Figures 109 and 110. An unusually shaped betel set box is shown in Figure 111. A particular style of betel tray and stand was produced in the northeastern part of Thailand (Isan). These were made of wood and often decorated with bone or horn in an inlay technique. The wooden surface was given a finish of a thin layer of black lacquer. Usually the tray contained several compartments to hold the different ingredients necessary for the betel quid (Figs. 112–114).

As with the other utensils, complete sets are slowly disappearing from modern rural and urban households (Fig. 115). Today betel sets and utensils are no longer produced except for the tourist industry where they are considered to be representative of the culture of past times. Modern lacquer boxes do not have the elaborate patterns and designs of their predecessors and are mostly crude objects of mass production.

Betel sets produced by Northern Thai hill tribes

Since some of the hill tribes in the mountains of Northern Thailand, mainly the Karen, Akha, Lahu and Lisu, also indulge in betel quid chewing some of them also produce sets to keep the betel quid ingredients. These mountain dwellers use principally only materials which are readily available to them: wood, bamboo or rattan. From an artistic point of view the sets lack the elegance and perfection that is found in those made by the Thai people. The hill tribe sets are fine examples of simple craftsmanship. Widely in use are the betel leaf, areca nut and tobacco containers produced by the Karen tribe (Fig. 116). This type of container has even found its way to the markets in the northern provincial town of Chiang Mai. Other examples of boxes and containers which are used by the Lahu (Fig. 117) and Akha (Fig. 118) reveal their simple charm.

As this chapter has shown, the large variety of accessories are more than just tools for those indulging in the habit of betel quid chewing and more than beautiful collectibles. They represent threads in the cultural tapestries of the East. To study and gain knowledge of them yields access to the history, art and social patterns of several million Eastern people.

Fig. 118.1: Cochin Chinese prince and attendant, and a betel set on the table close to the elbow of the prince.

Fig. 118.2: The queen mother of Cambodia after a photograph of M Gsell. A betel set is seen on the left side of the print.

11. *Miang* Chewing in Thailand

Northern Thai people consider the use of *miang* (pickled or fermented tea) a typical northern trait. In Northern Thailand at *khantok* dinners served to accentuate and perpetuate old Northern customs one makes a special point of serving and chewing *miang*. Also when visitors come or when the family is sitting together the *miang* is passed around. Other items are added to the quid. One of the most frequent additions is coarse salt. Sugar, ginger and fried or roasted pig skin may also be added to the chew. Each person takes a pinch of the fermented leaves, rolls it up into a wad and chews it. Both men and women chew *miang*, often on a daily basis. Cigars, usually the local so-called *khi yo* cigars, are commonly smoked while *miang* is chewed. A *khi yo* is made of approximately equal quantities of home-grown, sun-dried Thai tobacco and the chopped bark of the *koi* tree (Steblud asper). These two ingredients are mixed and wrapped in a dried—and often ironed—banana leaf which is then rolled and tied to give a gently tapering cigar about 14–20 cm long and 1–2 cm in diameter. It is said that *miang* chewing enhances the pleasure of smoking. The *miang* quid is partly chewed, partly sucked until it has lost its juices and becomes loose and pulpy whereupon it may be swallowed or more commonly discarded. The origin and evolution of the use of *miang* is not clear. In his article, "Miang: Fermented tea in North Thailand", LeBar (1967) stated that *miang* chewing seemed to be limited to the area of Burma, Thailand and Laos. In fact, the production of fermented tea seems to be even more limited, being restricted to the hills stretching across from the Shan States to Northwestern Laos. Several hill tribes such as the Meo and Karen indulge in *miang* chewing (Reichart et al., 1987). However, they seem to have adopted this habit from highland farmers of Northern Thai origin. Production of fermented tea is also recorded for the hill dwelling Palaung of Burma and the Lamet of Laos.

An inscription dating from AD 1500 in Wat Phra That Hariphunchai in Lamphun (Northern Thailand) contains probably one of the earliest records of the existence of *miang*. Dr Penth (1990) has kindly supplied us with the following information concerning this:

> The king of Chiang Mai and his royal mother built and liberally equipped and stocked a scripture library at Wat Phra That Hariphunchai in Lamphun. For the upkeep of the library, the king made several donations which were subject to a number of provisions. One of the provisions was to set apart a certain money item to form a fund for loans with the interest to be used for expenses for areca and *miang* (*mak miang*).

Several travellers to Northern Thailand have mentioned the habit of *miang* chewing. In 1912 a German botanist, Hosseus, described the habit of *miang* chewing in his account of an expedition to Northern Siam:

> Eine der sofort ins Auge fallenden Äußerlichkeiten ist die charakteristisch "geschwollene Backe" der Lao. Während die Siamesen Betel kauen und dadurch Zähne und Mund verunstalten, haben die Laoten ein anderes Anregungsmittel, Tee und Salz, das im Mund zusammen verarbeitet wird. Dieses Mischung wirkt anregend auf die Leistungsfähigkeit des Menschen, so daß auch Europäer, die hier draußen leben, oft daraus buchstäblich neue Kraft saugen.

Also le May referred to *miang* chewing in his book, *Asian Arcady* (1926): "After the curry and rice betel nut is chewed and this is followed sometimes by '*miang*', a species of wild tea which is also chewed in small balls like a quid of tobacco".

Apart from boxes in which the fermented tea leaves are kept (see Fig. 101) the practice of *miang* chewing is not associated with the use of special utensils such as those for betel quid chewing which are described in the previous chapter.

The production of *miang*

Miang is produced from the leaves of the same species of bush (Camellia sinensis L.) that produces leaves for brewing tea. Wild tea bushes grow naturally in Southeast Asia at altitudes between 800 and 1,100 metres. *Miang* tea plantations or orchards, thought to have been introduced from the southern part of China, are found in Chiang Mai province at Mae Hong Son, Bong Yang, Fang and the Doi Chiang Dao area. There are, however, according to Thompson (1967), some linguistic indications that the Chinese first obtained the tea plant from the Thai people.

The *miang* industry in Northern Thailand is mainly a peasant monoculture, based on individual family units. According to Chotisukharat, 1962, there were *miang* plantations in Chiang Dao, Mae Taeng, San Pathong and Phrao. Although it is not known how many people and families were then involved in the production of *miang* in the Papae district of Chiang Mai there were about 100 factories producing *miang* in approximately 15 villages. The yearly production of one factory amounted to 30,000 *khams*. A *kham* is a quantity of fermented tea leaves in a bundle the size of a fist, held together by a piece of bamboo string (Fig. 119). Tea leaves which are suitable for the preparation of *miang* are harvested from April to November. While leaves for *miang* quid production are approximately six weeks old those for tea consumption are usually much younger. According to Chotisukharat one bush can be picked four times a year. The first picking is called the first growth of the leaves, the middle picking is the second growth of the leaves, the last picking comprises the leaves that grow after the second. Then there are the dew leaves, the leaves that grow by moisture from the dew early in winter. The pickers carry with them bags and baskets as well as *tok*, the material for binding the leaves. The leaves are formed into a cube about 10 cm x 10 cm in size and tied with a string of bamboo (*tok*).

After the fresh *khams* have been prepared they are put into a basket made of bamboo which can hold about 55 kilograms. These filled baskets are then put over a charcoal fire (*hai*) and the *khams* are steamed with boiling water for one to one and a half hours (Fig. 120). The steamed *miang* is then removed from the basket and spread out on a bamboo net in the open to cool. After having cooled for at least three hours the *miang* is repacked into a bamboo basket. This process from harvesting to packing into the baskets must be completed in one day. If this is not done the leaves will change their colour, resulting in an inferior quality of *miang*. The *miang* thus produced is called *miang faht* and does not need further fermentation. *Miang* submitted to fermentation is called *miang som*. After having undergone the steaming procedure the *khams* are tightly packed into baskets using several layers of banana leaves to make them airtight. For fermentation these baskets were formerly buried in the ground and left there for about one month. Recently, cement tanks have been introduced as fermentation containers. After the tank has been completely filled with *khams*, soil and stones are used to seal the containers. After fermentation the *khams* are taken out of the cement wells or baskets and then packed into smaller bamboo baskets. About 100 *khams* are usually packed into a *ka-taw* basket. These baskets are lined by either a plastic sheet or several layers of banana leaves. A bamboo lid is placed on top of the basket and fixed by bamboo clamps which are hammered into the upper layers of *miang*. *Miang* packed in this way can be kept for at least 15 months without undergoing changes in colour or taste. Two sizes of the bamboo baskets are known, the larger one called *tang*, taking up to 200 to 240 *khams* (75 to 80 kilograms), and a smaller one called *ka-taw* or *taw* or *puey-law*. This basket contains about 100 *khams* of approximately 20 kilograms (Figs. 121, 122).

In 1967 LeBar reported that the price of one *kham* of *miang* in Chiang Mai was 0.75 Baht. The price in the jungle was about 300 to 400 Baht per 1,000 *kham*. In 1989 the price for *miang faht* at a factory in Papae district

Fig. 119: Miang *as it is sold in the markets, with the characteristic strip of bamboo holding the kham together (Chiang Mai, Thailand).*

Fig. 120: In the process of miang production, fresh tea leaves contained in large baskets covered by conical lids are steamed on an open fire (Papae, Chiang Mai province, Thailand).

Fig. 121: Basket viewed from above filled with tightly packed khams of miang. Each kham the size of a fist is bound with a strip of bamboo (Papae, Chiang Mai province, Thailand).

Fig. 122: Baskets containing miang packed for the process of fermentation (Papae, Chiang Mai province, Thailand).

Fig. 123: Quid of miang *with added coarse salt ready to be chewed.*

was 2.40 to 3.20 Baht per *kham*, for *miang som* it was about two Baht per *kham*, the standard price for a *kham* of *miang* in the markets of Northern Thailand.

LeBar (1967) had the impression that in North Thailand the use of *miang* was more widespread than the use of the betel quid. Although LeBar was of the opinion that *miang* chewers usually do not indulge in betel chewing both habits may in fact be practised simultaneously by one person (Reichart et al., 1988). According to the workers at a Papae *miang* factory Northern Thai start chewing *miang* at the age of six. However, field studies (Reichart et al., 1988) showed that today only the older generation indulges in *miang* chewing (Figs. 123, 124). The average consumption is three quids per day, usually after meals. When receiving guests a householder offers them *miang*, nicely packed in fresh banana leaves, together with *khi yo* cigars (Figs. 125, 126). It is considered common courtesy to offer *miang* to visitors in the home. When individual *miang* chewers were asked why they chewed *miang* a common answer was that it revives one's spirits, or it is like drinking coffee. A *miang* quid is also used as a kind of pick-me-up, as on a tiring walk (LeBar, 1967). It is believed that *miang* aids digestion and reduces fatigue, the latter effect probably caused by the quite considerable caffeine content. It is said that *miang* has such a stimulating effect that it enables men to continue working even without food. The practice of *miang* chewing may lead to a

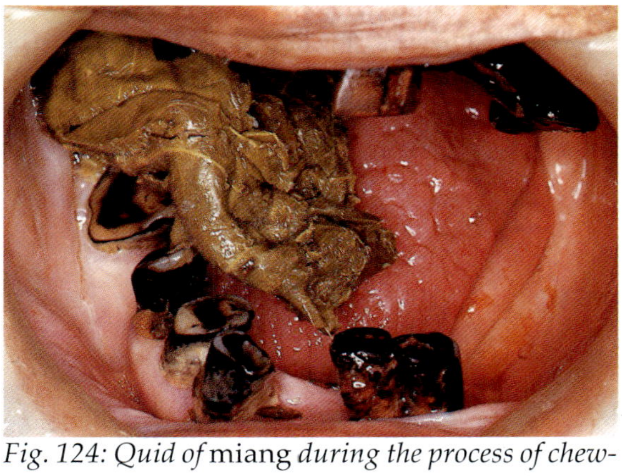

Fig. 124: Quid of miang *during the process of chewing. The black colour of the teeth shows that this person is also a betel quid chewer.*

Fig. 125: Small banana leaf basket as used during burials and other ceremonies. The small 4 cm by 2 cm packages contain miang and are offered to guests (Chiang Mai, Northern Thailand).

Fig. 126: Woman smoking khi yo cigar and chewing miang (Sankamphaeng, Chiang Mai, Thailand).

kind of habituation, but true addiction is not likely to develop.

In an analysis of *miang* production Keen (1978) came to the conclusion that the likely decline in per capita consumption of *miang* would significantly reduce future market prospects. In a survey conducted in 1970 and 1971 it was shown that all Northerners over the age of 25 used *miang*, but that only just over half of the younger group used it, the changing tastes of younger people most probably being the underlying cause. It was interesting to note that of 132 people of different age groups who were interviewed 80 stated that they disliked the taste or smell, 49 were unfamiliar with it, while two regarded it as too expensive or old fashioned. As Keen suspected, perhaps other refreshers such as chewing gum are now competitors.

Unlike betel quid chewing the habitual use of *miang* alone seems not to produce any adverse effects on the oral mucosa. However, the vast majority of *miang* chewers do in fact practise other habits, with betel quid chewing, cigar and cigarette smoking and alcohol consumption being predominant co-habits, all of which have a known association with oral precancerous or cancerous lesions. While *miang* chewing probably has no local side effects, it has been shown to have significant effect on the thiamine status of the body. Thiamine (vitamin B1) deficiency, which leads to beriberi, may develop as a result of chewing *miang*; this is due to the presence of the so-called anti-thiamine factor in the tea leaves (Vimokesant et al., 1974).

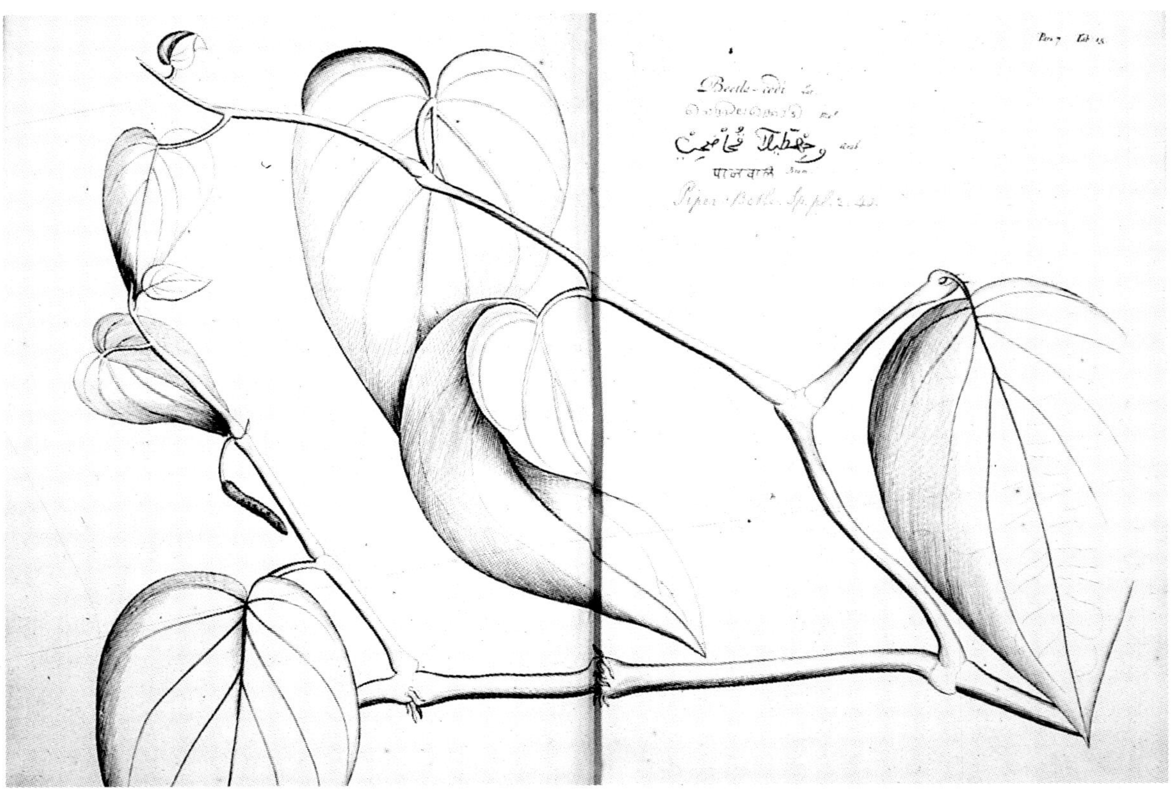

Fig. 127: Piper betel as published in Horti malararici pars septima de verii generis fructibus scandentibus; etc. *by van Rhede tot Draekestein, H., Amsterdam, 1688, Tab. 15.*

Fig. 128: The areca nuts on the tree, on the ground and betel vine creeping around the palm tree. Linschoten, seventeenth century, collection D. Ande, Bangkok.

References

Amranand P. *Siamese Pottery*. Thai Farmers Bank, Bangkok, 1986.

Anonymous. The Betel Tree. *The Bangkok Calendar For The Year of Our Lord 1864*, pp. 87–92. Bangkok, 1864.

Ashabranner B. & M. Brass boxes of the Southern Philippines. *Arts of Asia* 1982; **12**: 129–135.

Balendra W. Symposium on oral diseases in tropical countries. *British Dental Journal* 1949; **87**: 83–87.

Bock C. *Temples and Elephants. Travels in Siam in 1881–1882*. First published in London 1884. Reprinted Oxford University Press, Oxford, 1986.

Boisselier J. *Malerei in Thailand*. W. Kohlhammer, Stuttgart, 1976.

Bowring J. *The Kingdom and People of Siam; with a Narrative of the Mission to that Country*. Vol. I. J.W. Parker and Son, London, 1857.

Brownrigg H. *Betel Cutters*. Edition Hansjörg Mayer, Stuttgart & London, 1991.

Brus R. The Royal regalia of Thailand. *Arts of Asia* 1985; **15**: 92–99.

Buddle A. Cutting betel in style. *Arts of Asia* 1976; **6**: 34–39.

Burton-Bradley B. G. Papua and New Guinea transcultural psychiatry: some implications of betel chewing. *The Medical Journal of Australia* 1966; **15**: 744–746.

Burton-Bradley B. Betel chewing in retrospect. *Papua New Guinea Medical Journal* 1978; **21**: 236–241.

Cayley-Webster H. *Through New Guinea and the Cannibal Countries*. Unwin, London, 1898.

Chakarvarti S. K., Dhiman J., Nagpaul K. K. Uranium trace analysis of a chewable betel-leaf preparation and tea leaves. *Health Physics* 1981; **40**: 78–81.

de Chaumont Ch. *Rélation de l'Ambassade de M. le Chevalier de Chaumont à la Cour du Roy de Siam*. Pierre Mortier, Libraire sur le Vygendam, Paris, 1686.

Chinnery E. W. P. Piper methysticum in betel chewing. *Man* 1922; **15**: 24.

de Choisy L'Abbé M. *Journal du voyage de Siam (1585–86)*. Duchartre & van Buggenhoudt, Paris 1930 (reprint).

Chongkol C. Jewellery and other decorative arts in Thailand. *Arts of Asia* 1982; **12**: 82–91.

Chotisukharat S. *Thiao Muang Nua Lae Watthanatham Pra Pheni Khong Muang Nua* (Tour of the North: Culture and Customs of the North). Odeon, Bangkok, 1962.

Chumpengpan P. *Gold Treasures of the Ayutthaya Period*. M. Bunwong Publisher, Bangkok, 1986.

Conklin N. The faithful companion of everyday life. *Sawaddi* 1988a; **July/August**: 22–29.

Conklin N. The beauty of betel boxes. *Sawaddi* 1988b; **Sept./Oct.**: 8–14.

Ettinger R. L. Dental health beliefs and practices in a group of Thai villagers. *Odontostomatologie tropicale* 1985; **8**: 13–18.

Finlayson G. *The Mission to Siam, and Hué, the Capital of Cochin China, in the Years 1821–2*. J. Murray, London, 1826.

Fraser-Lu S. *Burmese Lacquerware*. The Tamarind Press, Bangkok, 1985.

Geiger W. *The Mahavamsa or the Great Chronicle of Ceylon* (translated into English). The Ceylon Government Information Department, Colombo, 1960.

Gode P. R. K. *Studies in Indian Cultural History*. Vol. I. Publication Committee, Poona, 1960.

Graham W. A. *Siam: Nature and Industry*. Vol. 1, Lords, Bangkok 1924.

Grabowsky F. Das Betelkauen bei den malayischen Völkern besonders aus Java and Borneo. *Internationales Archiv für Ethnographie* 1888; **1**: 188–191.

Hartwich C. *Die menschlichen Genussmittel*. Leipzig, 1911.

von Hesse-Wartegg E. *Siam, das Reich der weissen Elefanten*. Leipzig, 1899.

Hobson-Jobson. *A Glossary of Colloquial Anglo-Indian Words and Phrases, and of Kindred Terms, Etymological, Historical, Geographical and Discursive.* Yule, H., Burnell A. C. (eds:) First published 1886, Calcutta. Reprinted 1986, Munshiram Manoharlal.

Hosseus C. C. *Durch König Tschulalongkorns Reich*, pp. 26 and 126, Strecker & Schröder, Stuttgart, 1912.

IARC Monographs on the Evaluation of the Carcinogenic Risk of Chemicals to Humans. Tobacco Habits other than Smoking; Betel-Quid and Areca-Nut Chewing; and some Related Nitrosamines. Vol. 37. IARC, Lyon, 1985.

Keen F. G. B. The Fermented Tea (*Miang*) Economy of Northern Thailand. In: *Farmers in the Forest. Economic Development and Marginal Agriculture in Northern Thailand*, eds. P. Kunstadter, E. C. Chapman and S. Sabhasri, pp. 255–270. The University Press of Hawaii, Honolulu, 1978.

Klebert B. K. The Lerche collection. Chewing betel through the ages. *Arts of Asia* 1983; **13**: 107–113.

Kohnen N. "Ein und dasselbe ist Lebendiges und Totes..." Die enthaupteten Mutterschaftsfiguren aus Sawankhalok. *Deutsches Ärzteblatt* 1982; **79**: 71–75.

Krenger W. Betel. *Ciba Zeitschrift* 1942; **7**: 2922–2952.

Kumnung K. Therapeutic use of betel quid ingredients (in Thai). *Agriculture Magazine* 1987; **4**: No. 47.

LeBar F.M. Miang: Fermented tea in North Thailand. *Behavior Science Notes* 1967; **2**: 105–121.

Le May R. *An Asian Arcady. The Land and Peoples of Northern Siam*. W. Heffer & Sons Ltd., Cambridge, 1926.

Le May R. *The Culture of South-East Asia. The Heritage of India*. George Allen & Unwin Ltd., London, 1954.

Lewin L. *Phantastica. Narcotic and Stimulating Drugs. Their Use and Abuse*. Reprinted from the first English edition of 1931 with a new foreword by Bo Holmstedt. Routledge & Kegan Paul Ltd, London, 1964.

Lewis P. & E. *Völker im Goldenen Dreieck*. Edition Hansjörg Mayer, Stuttgart, 1984.

Locke C. J. Betel nut sets. *Arts of Asia* 1976; **6**: 25–29.

de la Loubère S. *The Kingdom of Siam*. First published 1688. Reprinted White Lotus, Bangkok 1986, pp. 23–24.

Lyons A. P. Notes on the Gogadara tribes of West Papua. *Journal of the Royal Anthropological Institute* 1926; **56**: 329.

Ministry of Commerce and Communications (eds.). *Siam, Nature and Industry*, Bangkok, 1930.

Millot J. *Inde et bétel. Objets et mondes*. Vol. 5, No. 2, Révue du Musée de l'Homme, Paris, 1965.

Morarjee, S. *Tambula: Tradition and Art*. Bombay, 1974.

Moser-Schmitt E. Sozioritueller Gebrauch von Betel in Indien. In: Völger, G.: *Rausch und Realität. Drogen im Kulturvergleich; Part 2. Materialienband zu einer Ausstellung des Rautenstrauch-Joest-Museums für Völkerkunde*. pp. 546–551, Köln, 1981.

Möller I. J., Pindborg J. J., Effendi I. The relation between betel chewing and dental caries. *Scandinavian Journal of Dental Research* 1977; **85**: 64–70.

Neale F. A. *Narrative of a Residence at the Capital of the Kingdom of Siam; with a Description of the Manners, Customs, and Laws of the Modern Siamese*. Office of the National Illustrated Library, London, 1852.

Newman T. R. *Contemporary Southeast Asian Arts and Crafts*. Crown Publishers, Inc., New York, 1977.

Penth H. Difficulties with inscription No. 1. *Journal of Siam Society* 1989; **77**: 91–100.

Penth H. Personal communication, 1990.

Penzer N. M. *Poison-Damsels and other Essays in Folklore and Anthropology*. Privately printed for Chas. J. Sawyer, Ltd., pp. 187–300, London, 1952.

Pindborg J. J. Illustration of betel (Areca) nut chewing in Sawankhalok celadon figurines from Thailand. *Journal of History of Medicine* 1973; **28**: 46–47.

Prunner G. *Meisterwerke burmanischer Lackkunst*. Hamburgisches Museum für Völkerkunde und Vorgeschichte. Im Selbstverlag, Hamburg, 1966.

Raghavan V., Baruah H. K. Areca nut. India's popular masticatory—History, chemistry and utilization. *Economic Botany* 1958; **12**: 315–325.

Reichart P. A., Lenz H., König H., Becker J., Mohr U. The black layer on the teeth of betel chewers: a light microscopic, microradiographic and electron-microscopic study. *Journal of Oral Pathology* 1985; **14**: 466–475.

Reichart P. A., Mohr U., Srisuwan S., Geerlings H., Theetranont C., Kangwanpong T. Precancerous and other oral mucosal lesions related to chewing, smoking and drinking habits in Thailand. *Community Dentistry and Oral Epidemiology* 1987; **15**: 152–160.

Reichart P. A., Philipsen H. P., Mohr U., Geerlings H., Srisuwan H. Miang chewing in Northern Thai villagers. *Tropical and Geographical Medicine* 1988, **40**: 39–44.

Reichart P. A., Schmidt-Westhausen A., Theetranont C. Oral cancer in Northern Thailand. *Experimental Pathology* 1990; **40**: 229–231.

Rickover R. M. *Pepper, Rice, and Elephants. A Southeast Asian Journey from Celebes to Siam*. United States Naval Institute, Annapolis, Maryland, 1975.

Rivers W. H. R. *History of Melanesian Society*. (2 volumes), Cambridge Univ. Press, Cambridge, 1914.

Rooney, D. F. *Betel Chewing Traditions in South-East Asia*. Oxford University Press, Oxford Singapore New York, 1993.

Sankaranarayanan R. Oral cancer in India: An epidemiologic and clinical review. *Oral Surgery, Oral Medicine and Oral Pathology* 1990; **69**: 325–330.

Segaller D. *More Thai Ways*. 2nd ed. Asia Books Co., Ltd., Bangkok, 1989.

Shaw J. Tak hilltop burial sites. *Arts of Asia* 1985; **15**: 95–102.

Sibunruang J. K. "Khun Chang, Khun Phèn". *La Femme, le Héros et le Vilain*. p. 151, Presses Universitaires de France, Paris, 1960.

Sinor P. N., Gupta P. C., Murti P. R., Bhonsle R. B., Daftary D. K., Mehta F. S., Pindborg J. J. A case-control study of oral submucous fibrosis with special reference to the etiologic role of areca nut. *Journal of Oral Pathology and Medicine* 1990; **19**: 94–98.

Smith M. *A Physician at the Court of Siam*. Country Life Limited, London, 1947.

Spinks C. N. *The Ceramic Wares of Siam*. The Siam Society, Bangkok, 1965.

Tennent J. E. *Ceylon. An account on the Island, physical, historical, and topographical .../ with notices of its natural history, antiquities and productions*. Vol. 1, pp. 112–115, 438–439. Longman, Green, & Roberts, London, 1859.

van Tent B. J. Drie "Kalkpotjes" uit het Verre Oosten van de Tijd rond 1500. Vereniging van Vrienden der Aziatische Kunst Amsterdam. *Mededelingenblad* 1983; **13**: 14–18.

Thierry S. *Le bétel. I. Inde et Asie du Sud-Est*. Supplement au tome IX, 3, d'Objets et Mondes, Revue du Musée de l'Homme, Paris, 1969.

Thompson V. *Thailand, the New Siam*. Paragon Book Reprint Corporation, New York, 1967.

Today's Agriculture magazine. Betel vine—easy to grow—fast to harvest—demand from foreign markets. Mong Korrs Karnpim. Vol. **2** pp. 16–21, Bangkok, 1982.

Tucker A. The betel-nut habit. *Sawaddi* 1984; **March/April**: 26–28.

Verwilghen F. Betel leaf holders. *Arts of Asia* 1985; **15**: 98–105.

Vimokesant S. L. et al. Effect of tea consumption on thiamin status in man. *Nutrition Reports International* 1974; **9**: 371–376.

Vimokesant S. L. et al. Effects of betel nut and fermented fish on the thiamin status of northeastern Thais. *American Journal of Clinical Nutrition* 1975; **28**: 1458–1463.

Völger G. *Südostasiatisches Silber-Sammlung Siegel*. Rautenstrauch-Joest-Museum, Köln, 1984.

Wenk K. *Die Ruderlieder in der Literatur Thailands*. Deutsch Morgenländische Gesellschaft. pp 129–130, Kommissionsverlag Franz Steiner GmbH, Wiesbaden, 1968.

Wenk K. *Studien zur Literatur der Thai. Texte und Interpretationen*. Band I. Gesellschaft für Natur- und Völkerkunde Ostasiens e. V. pp. 17 and 121, Tokyo and Hamburg, 1982.

Williams F. E. *Orokaiva Magic*. Oxford University Press, London, 1930.

Williamson R. W. *The Mafulu People of British New Guinea*. Macmillan, London, 1912.

Wirz P. *Die Gemeinde der Gogodara*. E.J. Brill, pp. 371–499, Leiden, 1934.

Wood W. A. R. *Consul in Paradise*. London, 1965.

Young, E. *The Kingdom of the Yellow Robe*. Archibald Constable, London, 1907.

de Young J. E. *Village Life in Modern Thailand*. University of California Press, Los Angeles, 1955.

Fig. 129: The areca nuts (lower part of print) and the betel leaf (right side, near the doorway). Linschoten, seventeenth century, collection D, Ande, Bangkok.